M●RTIFIED

Real Words. Real People. Real Pathetic.

MORTIFIED
Real Words. Real People. Real Pathetic.

DAVID NADELBERG

Associate Editors

NEIL KATCHER
KRISTA LANPHEAR
SCOTT LIFTON
GIULIA ROZZI

SSE

SIMON SPOTLIGHT ENTERTAINMENT
New York   London   Toronto   Sydney

SSE

SIMON SPOTLIGHT ENTERTAINMENT

An imprint of Simon & Schuster, Inc.

1230 Avenue of the Americas, New York, New York 10020

SIMON SPOTLIGHT ENTERTAINMENT and related logo are trademarks of
Simon & Schuster, Inc.

Designed by Yaffa Jaskoll

Manufactured in the United States of America

First Edition 10 9 8 7 6 5 4 3 2 1

Portions of Lori Gottlieb's "The Rodeo Drive Diet" appear in her book *Stick Figure: A Diary of My Former Self*, published by Simon & Schuster, 2000.

Library of Congress Cataloging-in-Publication Data

Mortified : real words. real people. real pathetic. / [edited] by David Nadelberg ;
associate editors, Neil Katcher ... [et al.]. — 1st ed. p. cm.

ISBN-13: 978-1-4169-2807-2

ISBN-10: 1-4169-2807-3

1. Teenagers' writings, American. 2. American wit and humor. 3. Adolescence—
Literary collections. 4. Anxiety—Literary collections.

I. Nadelberg, David. II. Katcher, Neil.

PS508.T44M67 2006

810.8'09283090511—dc22

2006013054

WARNING:

"THIS NEWS I'M GONNA BE WRITING ISN'T FUNNY
AND I SWEAR TO GOD IF <u>ANYONE</u> IS READING THIS
YOU BETTER SHUT IT NOW
CUZ THIS IS <u>NONE</u> OF YOUR BUSINESS!"

—Jennifer McDonnell, age thirteen, 1989, actual diary

THANGST!

Lots of people helped *Mortified* grow up from being a scrawny little runt to being . . . a scrawny little runt with a book deal. They even taught us to say our proper "pleases" and "thanks yous." So here are a few people and places that *Mortified* totally like-likes now and forever.

The First Willing Victims

Mathew Harawitz, Jennifer McDonnell, Kerri Pomarolli, Sascha Rothchild, Giulia Rozzi, Johanna Stein, and Elizabeth Zamos (who chickened out for the world's coolest reason)

The Mortiphiles

All Things Considered, Sara Alloco, Joe Amario, *Boston Globe*, Brandy Barber, Drew and Keleigh Biehlanphear, Judy Blume (Patron Saint), Paul Coogan, Diane Cook, Andrew Covell, Terra Chalberg, *Chicago Tribune*, Daily Candy, Shay Degrandis, Lauren Dolgen, Gordon Eick, Missy and Brian Evans, Jane Feltes, Annette Ferrara, Flavorpill.net, Lauren Forte, David Fox, Zoe Friedman, Eddie Gamarra, Gothamist, Gawker, William Hall, Angel and Kevin Herlihy, Lauren Horwitch, Gitta Hughes, Ina Jaffe, *Jane* magazine, Yaffa Jaskoll, Neil Katcher, Daniel Kirschner, LA.com, *Los Angeles Times Magazine*, Jen Lakin, Krista Lanphear, Jason Levine, Lauren Lexton, Gabe Lewis, Scott Lifton, Jenny Ruth Myers, Bob Nadelberg, Judy and Stephen Nadelberg, NPR, Patrick Price, Joe Reynolds and the M Bar staff, Tom Rogan, Sam Rosen, Davy Rothbart,

Rob Sachs, *San Francisco Bay Guardian*, Jeni Seidler-Pro, Craig Silverstein, Adam Soldinger, Julie Snyder, Kim Stenton, Mike Stern, Drew Tappon, Craig Taylor, *This American Life*, Heather Van Atta, Debbie Varshawsky, Liz Wise, Julie Wolfson, Amy Woods, Margy Yuspa, our fans, our cast, all those people who blog about us, and anyone who courageously submitted stuff.

Thanks to all them, we've got angst in our pants.

INTRODUCTION
HOW I GOT MORTIFIED

In the days before blogs, people transcribed their everyday events with ancient tools known as *pens* and *paper*. Back then, private thoughts were not written to serve as public spectacle. Rather, they were intensely guarded keepsakes, hidden under beds, locked in cabinets, or buried in the back of closets. These were called diaries . . . or if they were owned by heterosexual males, journals. To their oh-so-sensitive authors, such books served as their confidante, their shrink, and in a few somewhat pathetic cases, their only friend.

I never actually kept a diary or a journal—at least not for more than three days. My older sister, Debbie, however, was a tad more prolific. And when she skipped off to college, I naturally snuck into her bedroom—as if pulled by some preteen tractor beam—and read her private thoughts. I got a voyeuristic thrill reading about her then-current crush or how Mom was being "such a total bitch and I don't care if she's really reading this right now." But the thrill became more sobering when I stumbled on some entries about . . . me. They weren't bitchy or whiny. They were concerned. I had apparently been having trouble at school and was depressed and, being a good sister, she was worried. And that's when the guilt set in, and I quietly closed her book forever.

The desire to read people's private thoughts is ingrained in all of us, though with specific devotion attributed to nosy little brothers. And while sneaking into my sister's room and reading her words without permission was wrong, our *hunger* for peeking into anyone's life with such detail is not. I've come to learn the reason behind this desire is more intimate than imagined. Simply put, these diaries, journals, notes, lyrics, poems, and letters are all windows into who we truly were . . . and still are. We are captivated by others' innermost musings because in them we spot our own awkward identities. Witnessing them, in all their startling clumsiness, we can't help *but* laugh.

In my mid-twenties, I dug up a wretchedly lame unsent love letter (included in this book) that I apparently wrote to a girl in high school. I shared it with my roommates, who took ruthless delight in hearing it read aloud. I figured other people were hopefully just as pathetic. Luckily, I was right.

Mortified began as way of unleashing once private words off the page and in front of live audiences. The first *Mortified* show was intended as a one-time event. I had no idea if it would be funny past the first five minutes. I was terrified people would find it a fleeting retro fix. After all, this wasn't exactly a proven formula. It was just something that entertained my friends. And hence, to ward off such criticism, the concept of the "diagraphy" was born—*Mortified*'s odd editorial process by which we assemble actual childhood words into unique autobiographical tales. The entries that appear in *Mortified* (either on stage or page) are not so much a collection of verbatim journals, but more like carefully selected "windows" into people's pasts.

We're often told that real life doesn't quite play out like a story. But through *Mortified*, I've learned that real life is *exactly* where all that classic story structure comes from. When the show debuted, audiences weren't just laughing. They were relating, even rooting for the "characters" as though they had been ripped from the pages of their own lives.

And thus, the little showcase of stunted youth began to grow up.

There's a safe distance between the kid who wrote this dreck and the adult who's reading it years later. And while *part* of the charm in reading other people's childhood writings is in laughing at their naïveté or hearing kitschy retro references, *most* of the appeal is simply because we desperately want these kids to come out okay. There's something sadly heroic about each of these entries. Even though I've never prayed to Jesus . . . or snorted coke between classes . . . or wrote love songs to girls who later became lesbians, I can't help but crack up when reading the accounts of people who did. You can't laugh at something without relating to it. No matter what your race, gender, generation, or social rank (jock, brain, rebel, insert remaining John Hughes characters here), we were all that *same* strange kid. We couldn't escape them then, and we certainly can't escape them today.

With the release of this book, those words finally find their way *back* home to the page. If there's something these entries echo, it's that it's simply tough to be kid. It's scary. It's exciting. It's freaky.

As kids, we don't ever think our voices are being heard. We feel small. Insignificant. What I find strangely comforting about this project is knowing that, even if it *is* a few decades late, someone's listening.

If I could apologize to the teenage version of my sister, I would tell her just this: It might not get easier. It might not get simpler. The drama may never end. But the good news is simple. You grow up. You survive. (So stop spazzing out about not wearing your hair gel when Brian walks by.) *You'll be okay.*

With this book, I hope to offer a snapshot of human history at its most hilarious and haunting.

Share the shame.

Dave Nadelberg
Creator-Producer-Angstologist
Mortified

NOTE TO THE READER

To protect the innocent, awkward, and angsty, many of the names, dates, places, and other identifying details listed in this book have been altered.

As is the nature of *Mortified*'s editorial process, portions of the original text have been altered and arranged for sake of narrative and clarity. However, in keeping with the spirit of authenticity, no new sentences were ever created or inserted by the editors.

In short, these kids really wrote this crap.

CONTRIBUTORS:

REWRITING ROMANCE

Alexa Alemanni

When I was fourteen I spent my summer at a musical theater camp, and I fell in love with a boy named Sam. He was from Milwaukee, and he played the clarinet. I was in love with Sam from the first day I met him, and I pursued him like crazy. Sadly, nothing ever happened. Finally, on the last night of camp the two of us stayed up the whole night talking. But still *nothing happened*.

Now, I was a pretty obsessive, neurotic teenager, and I firmly believed that with enough hard work I would always get what I wanted, including Sam.

So I started writing him letters. But not just *any* letters. They had to be perfect. I wrote draft upon draft upon draft of letters to Sam and kept them all in a journal.

One last thing: He had a girlfriend the whole time we were at camp, before camp, and after camp. Her name was Jenna.

LETTER ONE

Dear Sam,

I was sitting at the bus stop in Denver and there was a man across the street . . . or maybe across a time zone . . . playing the clarinet. Coincidence? I think not.

Alexa

HIS REPLY
Alexa,
Hey. Hope all is well. Write back whenever.
Sam

MY REPLY, DRAFT ONE (DISCARDED)
Dear Sam,
What is up? It's been FOREVER since we last talked! Greetings from good old Denver, Colorado. It's sunny and seventy-five here, in November. Isn't that just crazy? What a great place to live. Hope you're okay.
Alexa

MY REPLY, DRAFT TWO (DISCARDED)
Dear Sam,
Glad everything is cool, I just figured there was too much snow to get to a mailbox!
Alexa

MY REPLY, DRAFT THREE *(SENT)*
Sam,
Good to hear from you! I was worried when you didn't write back right away. I thought you'd vanished into "the black hole of Milwaukee"! Ha ha!
Alexa
P.S. When are you in Denver again?

HIS REPLY

Alexa,

Might be there for New Year's. Who knows. Keep it real.

Sam

MY REPLY TO HIS REPLY, DRAFT ONE (DISCARDED)

Sam,

Do you remember this place? Do you remember the touch of synthetic fabric? Or the touch of your hand on my face? Do we not speak of such things? Do you think of me? What do you see? Behind my mask, my untouchable heart? *Maybe I can show it to you sometime.*

Alexa

MY REPLY TO HIS REPLY, DRAFT TWO (DISCARDED)

Sam,

And so I write, and prepare myself to wait for you to respond. But the time in waiting for you to write back to me is *nothing* in comparison to the time we'll have together in the future. And so I wait. If wedding dresses and curly haired children appear in my imagination, I can allow them to linger *ever so briefly*.

You're the first time I've played MASH, *not* cheated, and had it turn out every way I dreamed it—with *you*. I had a dream that you played the clarinet for me when I couldn't sleep, and our daughter had beautiful hair.

I guess her name can never be Jenna. I swore I'd never even say her name. How often do you?

Alexa

MY REPLY TO HIS REPLY, DRAFT THREE (DISCARDED)

Dear Sam,

Dreaming of you always. Or as "Marion the Librarian" sings to the stars not knowing her "music man" is so near: "But my love depends on a wish and a star—so long as my heart doesn't know who you are." But *I* know who you are. Sweet dreams be yours, dear. I will set your world on fire.

MY REPLY TO HIS REPLY, DRAFT FOUR *(SENT)*

Sam—

Great to hear from you! Are you excited for Thanksgiving? I am! I forgot if I asked you if you're going to be here for Christmas or New Year's. Silly me! Ha ha! Hope you're well.

Alexa

HIS REPLY

Alexa—

I'll be back in Denver around Christmas time. Not to sure yet. Will you be there? . . .

Sam

MY REPLY TO HIS REPLY TO MY REPLY, DRAFT ONE (DISCARDED)

Sam

"WILL YOU BE THERE? . . ." can only imply "I hope you still are so I can see you." *Will you be there?* is solely polite. *Will you be there? (with an ellipsis)* is in reference to my other plans. The choice of the word "will" implies an urgency of "I hope you will

still be there." That was a big clue, Samuel. You gave me a big hint right there. Did you mean to do that? I think you meant it. Ellipses after a question mark are always strategically placed. They are *never* unintentional. A question mark *ends* the sentence. Extending it with an ellipse is a *choice*! Good work, Samuel.

Alexa

MY REPLY TO HIS REPLY TO MY REPLY, DRAFT TWO (DISCARDED)

Sam,

I dreamed I came to Milwaukee for Christmas. We went to your parents' house. I helped your mother with the cranberry sauce and you told your father you thought you were in love. *Who have I become because of you?* A love-struck Juliet who writes nightly in a Five-Star notebook about her hopes and dreams of future happiness with her one and only Milwaukee love? Who, who, who have I become?

I cut my thumb when slicing a lemon today because I was thinking about you. You saw that coming, didn't you, Samuel? My eyes burn to see you, the way my finger burns from the acid of the citrus fruit.

MY REPLY TO HIS REPLY TO MY REPLY, DRAFT THREE (DISCARDED)

Sam,

I wish you would say: *Come to Milwaukee.* Three words. The most *beautiful* words. Come, come here, here, not there, near me, plead, come, command, demand, no choice, you must come, Milwaukee, unpleasant and harsh, yet contains *you*, dichotomy of sensory responses, waukee, extended k's long e's exuberant exhales, sighs of breath, orgasmic release, or softly caressed. A simple, powerful, mind-tingling, over-the-top phenomenal, frightening romantic and delicately dynamic suggestion. The possibility of anything—a verb, a noun and a period. It could be anything in the world. *Just ask it! Please!*

NO DRAFT FOUR, WROTE A POEM INSTEAD

She grasps the empty air for solace, comfort, and understanding
air, cold, void, biting air is none of those things
a solitary melody, played on a solo "Saigon-ian" saxophone.
I will never be your Miss Saigon, but I still believe I am your "Kim".
You are "Chris". Why must you have an "Ellen"—Jenna—call her what you will!
Unforeseeable chambers.
A window, a door, a river, a time zone, a saxophone . . . *except you play the clarinet.*
Days lost, chin knocks, here's looking at you kid,
Memories burn under summer skies,
Touch, touch is not a solitary sense.
An abduction, seduction, suspension of disbelief,
oh to be Cary Granted off my feet.
But I remain lost on the shores of Egypt.
The pyramids of Manhattan point to nothing.
You are *nowhere* to be found.

MY REPLY TO HIS REPLY TO MY REPLY, FINAL DRAFT (SENT)

December 28th 1995

Dear Sam,
The truth is . . . I really like you.

ADULT ME SAYS

And he never replied.

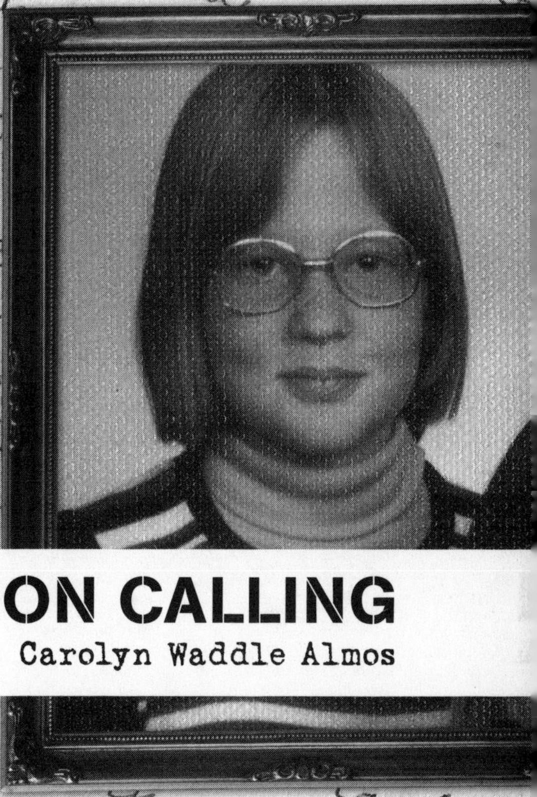

LONDON CALLING

Carolyn Waddle Almos

I grew up in a small town where the big cultural event was the rodeo. I always suspected I may have been dropped there by accident.

Then, when I was thirteen, a thrilling thing happened: My father got a sabbatical to study in Britain. I went with my parents and my sister, Susie, to Europe for six months. First we traveled around the continent and visited the house where Anne Frank hid from the Nazis. Then we stayed in London for three and a half months.

In that short amount of time, much like Eliza Doolittle, I underwent an amazing transformation. I slowly began to assume my true identity—a plucky British heroine from the 1940s.

October 2, 1981

I suppose the reason I'm writing this is because of Anne Frank. I love Anne Frank. I really do. What a courageous talented soul she was! I've only read two books on Anne Frank, but I hunger for more. I've been thinking a lot about this diary today. I suppose because it almost seems like an adventure. "Being like Anne Frank." Oh Anne how I wish you were here right now. It is horrible having an obsession that can never be satisfied!

P.S. Susie got two letters in the post today. I'm green with envy!

October 5

I must explain about my abrupt ending last night. You see, I can't bear to be the last one to sleep. Alas, I rush into bed. I suppose it has something to do with my insomnia. C'mon Carol get happy! I, Carol Waddle, do promise not to think of dreary, depressing things!

October 15

Tonight I went to my first Templars Drama Club meeting. I would like to do a drama. A social drama. I'd like a part for a young woman. I can't play most children's parts, and most seem to be quite stupid, as adults apparently have forgotten, or never could, understand children. Children are so wonderful. I want always to be a child, yet at the same time, I want to be an adult.

October 22

Did I tell you? I'm going to work on costumes for "Blithe Spirit" for the Templars. They asked me about it as though I must be so brave to take on the work. How I dote on each little thing I do in drama! It's not a chore, but a privilege doing the thing I love!

November 17

The police came to check our garage for IRA bombs. I found out about laboratory animals and dogs in the Philippines. After they had the dogs on TV, I went upstairs and sobbed the tears I had been holding during the film. They do horrid things to them! Please God, can't you do anything? The police checked the garage because the IRA (as you probably know) is blowing things up like crazy. And killing! And what's worse, the jerks start killing Catholics simply because the IRA doesn't like Protestants! Oh, FUCK the IRA! I absolutely loathe those murdering bastards. I'm sorry, but I hate them so much. And those animal killers too. What is wrong with people?

December 8
Oh, I feel happy today. I just finished a marvelous book. And it's SNOWING! The house is very bright. I have hung up the decorations Susie and I have made. Also, the red and green paper chain for the tree is finished. This afternoon we are going to see "Cats." Oh Glorious Day!

December 15
I can't believe what is happening in Poland. Martial law on Sunday. Today Walesa under house arrest. How can I save the victims? I can't take it anymore. I am going crazy. I have a nasty temperament and am miserable.

"One of us is crying"—ABBA

December 24
Now it is Christmas Eve. I'm glad I'm not depressed like last year. Shit. Somebody just clubbed some foxes with clubs on TV. I hate fox hunters. I loathe them. Cruel people. I'm not kidding, they should be put in jail. And I'll be damned if I don't try to stop hunters.

December 29
We just watched a heartwrenchingly sad movie called "Day

of the Dolphins" starring George C. Scott. At the end the two dolphins (who could speak) were let go by the scientist, George C. Scott. He had to, or they would be in danger. But as they left, Alpha and Beta were calling "Pa!" and "Ma!" and I wanted to bawl like a baby, but the tears slid down my cheeks silently. So you assume the dolphins are safe at the end (oh I hope! I couldn't bear the sadness if they weren't). It touched me in such a way, that even now my heart aches to think of it!

January 1, 1982

I am so very tense and short tempered. I constantly have to do dramatic limbering-up exercises to keep calm and from screaming. But I want to scream and I need to scream. I remember (to change the subject) a while ago when Jenni was staying overnight. We were playing RISK and Jenni said that when she played she always put yellow in Poland because they were yellow!

I said, "Jenni, how can you say that? These brave people are fighting for their freedom!" She shrugged it off. I will *always* remember her stupidity.

January 11

This is the last day of my fabulous Europe trip. But I will come back. After all, I'm only 13 and travel being as easy as it is today. Here I discovered Anne Frank. If I had a choice of one person I'd like to meet it would be her. Never to be. We could have been friends I imagine.

Well, goodbye Europe. It's been great. We'll have to get together again sometime.

really good today- I was
that this morning but I thought it s
I am cold and I look swell. I thin
much mascara on also. Does m
coo- "chesty!"
Guess who
she's so gross- Nov
I guess he doesn't kno
I wouldn't go back
is being a bi
does think he
was burnt! so ba
what does she th

I think he looks good- I mean he's re
I think I'll tell

PASSING NOTES
Anne Altman

you do look good too I like
this skirt on you a wicked lot.
I look swell! I don't think
it is to "chesty" eith
say she liked
start?

I grew up in a small town on Boston's North Shore. Like the majority of my sixth-grade peers, I was a typical naive nerd. Yet when the grade schools merged in junior high, I gained entrée to the "popular group" somehow. The cool kids "dated" and "partied," and I was determined to maintain a firm grip on this sudden popularity by constantly communicating with my new friend Melissa. She was exceptionally nice and smart for a cool girl, and she had the latest scoop on all the boys.

My mother once commented on my popularity, and I replied, "Yeah, well, it might look easy, but it's a lot of hard work, Mom." These notes, passed between me and Melissa (aka Mel and Melly) in eighth and ninth grade, chronicle my tenacious struggle.

Had I been that dedicated to my schoolwork, I'd have gone to Harvard. Right, Mom?

New Note

Mel, how are ya? Doesn't my hair look gross? I didn't curl it. You look really nice today! Now tell me, do I have too much lipstick on? 'Cause if it looks slutty I'll take it off. It's just a <u>little</u> bright! Anyway, what's up? Cassie doesn't want me to go to the dance because she doesn't have any money. She wants to save for Florida; she'll never save it.

Once she gets the money for babysitting, she'll blow it on gum. I'll go to that dance for the hell of it, I mean, what the heck? Nothing else to do! Who does Glenn like? I wonder if he is gonna bug you today about me! The word Math makes me sick. I don't understand it. It's way too hard. You see, every time Glenn sees Courtenay, he makes SURE that she knows that he's around. He'll go "HI COURTENAY!" wicked loud and she'll go "Hi, Glenn!" She knows he likes her.

Anyway, so then like if we are with a bunch of kids talking, like say me, Glenn, Courtenay, Alyssa, etc., he'll look at Courtenay, smile huge and wave—I mean give me a break. It's so damn obvious. What a shit. He doesn't have to like me but he CAN'T like someone else. It's weird though, in a little teeny way it seems that he likes me, just a <u>little</u> bit, hardly noticeable. Well I don't know. Then again, I bet he doesn't. Ah forget it. Look at this! I wrote a whole damn page about this queer! Write back!

AA

P.S. Marc is a good kid. You still like him, don't cha— I can tell, I'm not too thick. I think he likes you a little too—and don't say he doesn't, cause he does. I saw him the other night talking to you . . .

New Note

Melissa,

Don't worry about Marc, it's not a big deal. Something will click, and the whole thing will be just nifty. Not with me though, the whole thing is a mess. Guess who Alyssa likes?! Glenn! I hate that bitch! She's <u>so</u> gross! I can't wait to see what happens at the end of today! I know he's going to ask her out.

Who does he like? I *like* him. But I don't know if I like him. but I don't hate him. I don't wanta like him! He hates Cassie. Cassie thinks he hates me too, but she's burnt because he doesn't—we were on the phone for like a 1/2 hour!

Write Back!

New Note

Mel,

I bet Cheryl said that, but she *does* exaggerate. A LOT. Kevin said Cassie was mouthing off wicked bad yesterday morning. She treats her Mom like shit and lies a lot. It's weird, I kinda want you to tell Glenn about me but I know it will wreck everything and then he will hate me 'cause he will never like me anyway. It's like I have cooties or something. I don't know, you could just ask him who he likes. I know he's gonna say Courtenay, that's what he always says, but who cares? Are you going on the field trip to Washington D.C.?

W/B!

New Note

Melissa,

How are ya? Cassie isn't in a bitchy *mood*, she's just a bitch. She's totally changed. I bet she gets smashed every weekend with the burners on the golf course. I'm never going there. Cheryl is pissed at her too. Glenn might get an idea I like him. He's wearing a brown sweater thing and he looks cute. The only reason I like him is 'cause when he's nice he's wicked nice to me and he's fun to talk to. I want him to know about me, but

I don't. you know? 'Cause I'm positive he'd rather have Alyssa over me, Courtenay over me, etc. . . . I'm gonna _die_ when he asks Alyssa out this week—which I _know_ will happen.

Write Back Definitely I'm Bored

New Note

Mel—

Of course that girl is a bitch. I mean, she's a senior! Even if she was the best kid in the world, she'd still be a bitch cause she's a SENIOR. Well, la—dee—da. You know? Are you still happy about Marc? That's good. How are you guys together? Fine? Good. Anyway, I really don't like Glenn anymore and I'm psyched.

Yesterday, I was at the park and Glenn said "Hi, Anne" once and then talked to some other kids and then Billy said to me "You always wear red!" and I go, "I know!" Then I went over and talked to him for about 1 1/2 hours! We went to Cindy's Superette and then he rode me home to my house—me on my bike and him on his bike. We were talking and talking about all this stuff—it was great! He's _SO_ cute! I ♥ him. He's so much better than Glenn—_cuter_ too.

W/B!!!

New Note

Mel—

How are ya? I'm okay. Anyway, did Marc leave for vacation? That's a bummer, huh? Do you still like him? Cassie was so burnt before the dance—how long is she going to be suspended for?

I warned her—I had a pretty good time at the dance. I still like Bill just a little—not too much—'cause I know he's never like me—he's too old. Anyway, he was at my house all weekend! Friday afternoon from 3-4 pm, then 6-7, then 8-12:45am. Then on Saturday he came over for about 2 hours (this is all to help me with my Halloween costume) then from 8-11 at the dance (he was a little drunk I think). Anyway, he called me last night. I called him back but he wasn't home. He said hi to me in the hall today, and that's it! Well, g/g, period's gonna end.

Love ya, Anne

W/B

New Note

Melly,

Hi buddy, how are you? I hope this day goes by slow. You see, I like Billy a lot and I want to see him around in school, if you know what I mean. Cassie's pants are too tight. Anyway, stop working on your report! You bitch! Cheryl hasn't started hers yet, neither has Doug. I think I have too much mascara on. I need a mirror. Did you break up with Marc? Is he in school? I wonder if Bill likes me. I doubt it very much but I don't know what to think you know, cause he's really nice to me . . . but he's got his own friends and stuff, I mean . . . he's a senior! I don't know, maybe he likes me as a friend but I like him more than that! Can't you tell?

Write Back!!!

ADULT ME SAYS

The following is a note I wrote for my eyes only, as a freshman after I believed Billy stomped on my heart.

New Note

Anne loves? Billy? Billy loves Heather! Heather is a gay fag ugly preppie! I hope Billy realizes that Heather is a gay fag ugly preppie soon!

In the meantime, Anne, who is awesome, beautiful, amazing wonderful and is better than Heather, but too good for Billy, will try to forget both of them for a long while and really try hard to get a nice kind, considerate handsome thin boyfriend! So BYE BYE BILLY and HEATHER, you both will be burnt in the end! Especially you, Heather, you fat-assed, zit-faced ugly queero 17 year old snobby preppie un-coordinated bitch! *You can't even dance!* Why don't you just do it right there on the gym floor in the middle of the dance? Huh? Are you glad you got rid of me, Billy? Huh? Good! I hate you too! I may be a freshman, but I have feelings! Why don't you just tell the whole world about this bitch and throw her picture around and shove it in people's faces! They don't care!

Nice 'do!

What did you cut it for Heather? Why don't you spend your whole life savings on this fat bitch! Spend the rest of your life with her you hypocrite! You are a snobby two-timing double hypocrite with NO CLASS whatsoever! And I do. And I am: losing weight, getting new clothes, being happier, being prettier, growing longer, blonder hair, getting a new boyfriend and getting BETTER grades! SO YOU ARE BURNT! Nice life, Billy, nice life. Give me a call sometime, and let me know how you're doing, you stupid stud.

So, ANNE LOVES???

Who could I like?

BYE BYE!

24

BAD ADVICE

Anonymous (author was honestly too mortified)

BAD ADVICE

I spent most of my high school years in honors classes, doing homework and socializing with friends of my similarly low social ranking. However, the summer before my senior year in high school, I managed to come out of my shell socially, even enjoying my first beer on a camping trip—yeah, I felt like the BWOC (big woman on campus).

So by the end of this truly wonderful summer, a close friend who had similarly undergone this social awakening and I wanted to share our newly *enlightened* way of stepping up the social ranks to other fellow "nerds with potential."

So we scouted out the perfect candidate and became obsessed with the idea of transforming him from nerd to popular boy. We decided to send an anonymous "letter of advice" to him in the mail as a sort of guide to how he, too, could make this social transformation to being cool.

In retrospect, its tone did not exactly have the feel-good vibe as intended.

Stan—

I really think you have the potential to be very good-looking, but you need some work to reach this point. This letter is in no way an insult, it is merely some helpful hints so that next year the girls will fall all over you.

Right now I think that you might repulse some girls. My hints are to make it so the girls will run towards you, not away.

1. You really need to get a little help with your acne. It is not that bad, but your face always seems to be greasy. No one wants to kiss a face that is dripping with oil.

2. You need to cut your hair. Right now your hair looks like the mane of a lion, which is in no way attractive. You need to cut your hair in such a way that the curls are not as obvious. A short haircut would take care of this. No matter what haircut you get, get one that will be above your neck! I think your hair is your biggest problem.

   Ask your hairdresser what he/she thinks would look good on you.

3. You need to dress better. No one likes to look over when you have your arm raised and see a yellow stain in your armpit, that is just plain disgusting! Look at how your fellow classmates dress. None of them wear obnoxious shirts that say things like "What part of no don't you understand?" Those shirts are just annoying.

   Start dressing a little more preppiesh (polo shirts, slacks, jeans, sweatshirts, etc.). Start shopping at stores like Nordstrom and look at what they sell. You won't see one of your t-shirts there—and that is good.

4. You need to lose a little weight. As you are now, you seem a little chunky. If you lose a little weight. I think you will look incredibly more attractive.

5. You also need to learn how to not be as obnoxious. You always make people cringe when you speak because you are so spastic. *Mellow*. Learn how to be mildly funny and sophisticated—not loud and annoying.

Please do not think this letter is meant to hurt your feelings. That was not my intent at all.

I want you to have a good senior year, and these hints are meant to help you achieve that. If you take my advice, you may actually get some interaction with decent females next year.

If you don't, girls will continue to think that you are the most disgusting thing on this earth. Believe me, you need to listen to this advice.

BRANDY VS. THE WORLD

Brandy Barber

When I was fifteen, I was convinced everyone was out to get me—my teachers, my parents, even my closest friends. It was Brandy vs. the World, and I couldn't understand why I was so persecuted.

I felt I had no choice but to act out against those who had wronged me. And when someone told me I was a really angry person, I was shocked. Me? A gentle, shy speech team geek? Me, who only wanted to be loved by her boyfriend and liked by her friends?

Upon reading my diary from back then, some insight as to who was *really* being persecuted may come to light. Hint: Not me, as much as I'd have liked to think so.

December 5, 1988

One of my best friends, Dan, broke up with my best friend Sara's older sister Leslie. I am supposedly the cause. Now I am the butt of all the hatred, even from Sara. I didn't do a single thing, I just acted like myself. I tried no advances, but now I'm supposedly a harlot. No one seems to care that I desperately need to be loved. It's all commotion over Leslie. Yeah, like she has trouble with boyfriends. I feel so utterly alone . . .

December 7, 1988

Dana T tried to irk me by writing "Trendy people who try to be unique get a life" on the chalkboard in the Speech Team room. Oh sure, I'd love to live yours!

December 8th, 1988

I think Dan and I actually have a relationship going on. We haven't held hands or anything, but we do hug a lot. Putting his arms around me just feels so . . . right. I feel like I could just stay there forever.

December 10th, 1988

Today was one of the strangest days of my life. First of all Mitch actually acknowledged my existence!!! Second, Dan asked me to Snowball and we kissed like, 5 million times. It was my first kiss today, even though I lied and said I kissed a boy from Washington named Mickey who lived by my Grandma. So I can't even tell anyone.

December 12th, 1988

I found out Colin and Tracey had a little "happy hands" fling on the bus back from the Holtville speech tournament. I don't think lower of either of them. After school me and Dan went to the mall and then to the beach. He asked me out, and the he mercilessly chewed on my ear. He finally took me home covered in sand no less!

December 14th, 1988

Tracey has betrayed me to Sara. Never trust the little pig

again!! Leslie, Sara's sister and aforementioned bitch, is on the rampage.

December 15th, 1988
Well tomorrow's my big Xmas couples party but I'm not too thrilled. Ugly bitch Dana still has her finger up her ass; hopefully she'll die.

December 16th, 1988
After school Dan and I went to his house where we make-out battled again, and as a result we were an hour late to my party. We picked up the foot-long sub, and then opened presents. I got a Jim Morrison book, earrings, an Edie Brickell CD, a Ministry tape, and candles. We got in the hot tub, and then my Mom came down and chased us around like a fool. I have postered my walls and lit some incense to my Mom's dismay. And to think, a year ago I liked dumb skater Peter S, was a total trendy fashion bop, and liked Tiffany and other Top 40.

December 18th, 1988
Sara and I stole Leslie's car and toilet papered Nick's house. We trashed it with toilet paper, garlic, vinegar, flour, rice, Woolite Rug Cleaner, coffee, honey, LaSuer peas, Vaseline, toothpicks in the keyhole of the cars, lice spray, and her brother's underwear with a love note. I found out Leslie spat on Dan's trench coat like 50 times and Sara let me wear it without telling me. So I spat all over Leslie's guitar and ruined her school picture with the Woolite.

December 23rd, 1988

I peeked at my presents and saw the White Album. Dana T has tried to avenge Nick by egging Leslie's car, but Sara and I laughed our butts off. Leslie treated me and Sara like we were crap and tried to imply that we were useless. I put bubble gum in all the pockets of her denim jacket.

December 24th, 1988

I am beginning to have aches, already I miss everyone who is around me. I know this year will be over before I'm ready for it. How will I survive without all these crazy people?!?

New Year's Resolutions 1989

1. Take dancing
2. Make love to: Mick Jagger, Keanu Reeves, Eric Stoltz, Christian Slater, Dave Gahan
3. Have illicit affair (as above)
4. Grow long nails

I will do at least 3 of these or GO BALD!!!

January 17, 1989

Today was the Cal State Fullerton Speech Tournament. I did minimally in my rounds. We went back to the hotel. Tracey and I hung out in Peter, Colin, and Mitch's room. I got to dance with Mitch. Mitch's friend Dave hung out: he had a red Camaro. When we went back to our room, I told Tracey we'd try to freak out dumb Meredith so we pretended to be secretly satanically meditating. Meredith prayed and bawled. Then we ditched her and snuck back to the guys' room. I developed a crush on Dave and kissed him—just real quick on the lips. He is hot and dresses New Wave and likes Depeche Mode—even though he is assistant manager at a Taco Bell and is Christian. I gave Pete a backrub and I really wanted to kiss him. We sang *Nights in White Satin*. And then on the way home Colin and I hugged. I really wanted us to kiss. I feel so close to everyone. Tracey and Pete kissed.

January 20, 1988
As of Jan. 19th, Pete and Sara BROKE UP. Friday was hell. Sara found out that Pete and Tracey kissed. The Snowball is tomorrow!

January 21, 1988
Snowball was kinda dead. We spiked the punch. Leslie was there and acted really mean to me. Sara bawled the entire time . . . then we went to Denny's and the beach. Dan yelled at me for flirting with Dave, Pete, Colin and John, Patty's date.

February 3rd, 1989
In Mr. Williams' history class I yelled out, "DaVinci was a necropheliac!" and "The Mona Lisa is a bisexual portrait!" We toilet papered the Wagner twins' house.

February 7th, 1989
I went to see a real shrink today because everyone thinks I'm crazy.

February 8th, 1989

Sara and I stole Spaniel/Daniel's car and drove around the teacher's parking lot. We almost hit a trash can and left skid marks. We almost drove out into the intersection but I got too scared. We are going to the Dead Milkmen concert tomorrow.

February 9th, 1989

I ditched 5th and 6th period to talk to Sara and Patty. We danced in front of a garbage truck and announced that we were mentally insane. Mitch got his mom's van and we drove to San Diego to see 91X's Laser Rock at the Planetarium. It was so great! Jon and I sang to Pink Floyd. I am very attracted to him and he broke up with Patty. We made a plan that someday we'd date. We went to the Distillery to go dancing afterwards. Only Mitch and I danced to his fave song, "My Posse's On Broadway."

Then we went to Denny's. Mitch rapped at Sara: "I'm gonna poke you but not with this fork." Sara threw her glass of water on him. I threw ice at everyone and crawled on the floor barking. Denny's will never be the same!

February 13th, 1989

I caused a near riot because of my antics in the school paper. I put "In Honor Of Ted Bundy" on a pizza discount ad. I went to Sara's house and we attempted to steal Harry's Maverick. Leslie discovered the ploy right off and ratted us out. We made Spaniel/Daniel drive us to the mall to get REM tickets. He left us in the car and we stole it again. I totally smashed another car and we almost got killed twice. Then Spaniel came back as black smoke started pouring out of the car. Later Pete came over alone and we talked for 2 hours . . . it was weird.

February 15th, 1989
Today we wrote essays, "No Good Deed Goes Unpunished." Mine was awful. We called the Wagner twins Kenny Loggins because they look like him.

February 18th, 1989
I spent the night at Sara's and we made Ex-Lax cookies and fed them to Leslie and her brother Bob.

February 22, 1989
Found out Max tried to kill himself with 40 nitroglycerin pills . . . I feel so sad, I cried for half an hour. I can't handle it. Note: Dan thinks I am self-centered. I wouldn't mind lighting him on fire. Sara and I tortured Christianly Christian Meredith and cut out her picture and put it on Garret's private parts in the Swim Team yearbook photo.

April 3rd, 1989
Mr. Driscoll is mad because in the April Fool's paper I published a joke article about Mr. Lents escaping from an asylum and we drew a swastika on his forehead like Manson and made a few Hitler references and now everyone's having a bovine birthright (a cow). He told the principal I snuck it past him. Ok.

April 17th, 1989
Everyone is still mad about the Mr. Lents thing. Pete made fun

of me. Patty and I watched "The Holy Grail" and "Wish You Were Here," then we all stayed up until 7:30 am on NoDoz and toilet papered Daniel/Spaniel's house with Maxipads, fabric cleaner, rice pilaf mix, urine, toilet paper, flea bomb fogger, shaving cream, Listerine, and flour. Dan gave me his swim team jersey. Patty and I went to see "Say Anything." It was dumb. We stole the PG-13 sign from the Plaza Camino Real Movie Theaters marquee.

April 18th, 1989
Patty, Teresa and I cranked the Wagner twins. They are so cute.

Dave Wagner: Hello? (breathes deep) Hello? (snorts impatiently) Hello?

(begins to hum vaguely)

Patty (yells while laughing): SAY SOMETHING!

Teresa (curtly): KENNY LOGGINS.

CLICK.

Patty told me that if she hated me, she wouldn't think I was pretty at all.

April 19th, 1989
Dan was all over me and he said, "Do you think we're going to end up sleeping together?" and I said, "NOPE!" Then he said it wasn't right because he was Christian.

Uh, Ok.

April 30th, 1989
Today my Mom talked to me about my having had sex. I think

I am going to start taking birth control pills to be safe. Sara is running for Vice President next year and we have New Order tickets.

June 13, 1989

School is over and my heart is broken. Dan is going to Cal State Fullerton in the fall and I am turning 16 in a month. Sara and I are closer than ever and Patty is moving to San Francisco because she got kicked out.

This has been the best year of my life. I don't know how I am going to live now. These are the best friends I'll ever be lucky enough to have!!!

THE PORN

Sara Barron

This is an excerpt from a little something I like to call "The Porn," a forty-plus-page story I wrote when I was twelve.

Obviously all of us go through puberty. But most people handle this onset of new feelings by playing doctor with a friend or learning how to masturbate in the bathtub under the faucet or something. Instead I went the road less traveled and worked it all out . . . by writing this epic dirty story.

The most interesting thing that I realized about "The Porn" when I reread it as an adult was that I didn't understand the concept of an orgasm. I got that you'd feel something down there, and I could tell that the feeling would build and build and that ultimately some sort of something would have to happen. But I simply could not conceive of *what* that might be. And so in my story, at the climactic moments, all the characters just . . . pee. They just pee everywhere and all over themselves as a means to release.

The lead character, Jenny Wilkinson, spent forty-plus pages wandering around her suburban town getting humped by varying high school boys. In this particular scene, Carrie (who I wrote would be played by Paula Abdul) and Jenny (who I wrote would be played by Christie Brinkley) are discussing their sexual promiscuities from the night before.

Carrie: OK, so exactly what happened.

Jenny: Well we got to his house and he took off his tee-shirt and put on black Umbros and said, "How easy is it to get those close off?" and I said, "Why don't you try and find out." So he took off my brassiere . . .

Carrie: You wore it?

Jenny: YES! Anyway, listen! So he's in black Umbro shorts with all his muscle and I'm in a black lacy underwear and brassier. So then he starts making out with me with tongue and ear biting.

Carrie: Wait a second. What are you doing all this time?

Jenny: I was rubbing my fingers through his luscious hair. Then we start violently and wildly humping while we roll over and french. We kept humping, incredibly. I want you to realize, this is no average hump. This is really pushing into each other. It's extremely satisfying. Then he says, "Now it's your turn to do something really wild."

Carrie: So what do you do?

Jenny: Well, I french him . . . completely. And then, while he's still doing that pushing hump that's so incredible, I take his pienis AND RUB MY FACE IN IT. Then I grab it in my two hands and rub it all over my body. Then I unhooked myself—

ADULT ME SAYS

Let me take a moment to explain the verb "unhooked." Before I actually encountered the glory that is the erect penis in real life, I thought it worked kind of like a hook. And so the woman would, like, hop on the hook and go for a ride.

Jenny: —and said, "Baby, it's your turn now." He goes back to that pushing hump that's so incredible, that violent french, and stares into my eyes. And in the middle of hotly and violently shoving our excited genitals together, since we were at our peak of heat, I was so excited, I peed on him. We both smiled slyly and he said, "oh yeah." And I cleaned it all up with the help of my boobs. Anyway, then he drove me home and we made out just with frenching, although we did lie on top of each other and I went inside and here I am.

Carrie: You're not lying to me are you? I mean, if you think about it, even for you and Mark that's pretty wild sex.

Jenny: I'm not lying.

Carrie: Yeah. I believe you. But anyways, how did it feel?

Jenny: Incredible. It felt real sexy, especially when he felt, squeezed and rubbed his hands on my vagina. It also felt really good when we were frenching and humping. How was your night with Brad? Did you do it?

Carrie: Yeah. Except it wasn't as wild as you and Mark.

Jenny: Tell me anyway.

Carrie: Well, Brad and I sat in his car and did it in the back seat while "Ice Ice Baby" was playing on the radio. He unzipped my leather jacket and frenched my boobs and squeezed my butt.

Jenny: Well, and I'm not saying this sarcastically, but Brad is pretty sexy.

Carrie: Yeah, I know. I'm still at his house. I can't wait for him to hump me again.

Jenny: Shit! All this talking has stirred me up. I was hoping Brad could come over to my house for awhile. Who should I call?

Carrie: You should call that kid Matt Divan. I hear they resumed Marcie's party. You could go there and reserve a room or something.

Jenny: That's an awesome idea. I'll call you later 'cause Brad will probably come to feel you up any minute.

Carrie: Probably. Bye.

Jenny: Bye.

ASIDE

So in the next scene Jenny Wilkinson goes right ahead and takes Carrie's advice and calls this character I made up named Matt Divan. Matt Divan was originally supposed to be played by Kirk Cameron.

Jenny: Hi. Is Matt there?

Matt: This is.

Jenny: Hi. This is Jenny Wilkinson. I'm not sure if you know me but I wanted to know if you wanted to go back to Marcie Glikstein's party with me?

Matt: Is this a prank call or is this really Jenny?

Jenny: This is really Jenny! Do you want to go or not?

Matt: Yes. Yes. Yes! I want to go!

Jenny: OK. I'll just wear, you know, some lacy underwear and bra and you should just wear some loose pair of shorts. I prefer Umbros. I'll pick you up 'cause I have this car and the seats are great for doing it. O.K, so I'll see you in five minutes.

Narrator: Five minutes later: Jenny drives up in front Matt's house and he appears in a pair of neon blue Umbros. Jenny

48

stands up in the driver's seat and waves. She is wearing a black very lacy and very revealing bra and string bikini bottom. She signals for Matt to come to her and she gets in the back seat.

Jenny: Come on! I'm getting antsy.
Matt: I'm coming.
Jenny: Okay. Have you ever had sex wildly before.
Matt: Yes. I've had it many times.
Jenny: Good. 'Cause you're with me now. And there is no such thing as regular sex. Only the wildly kind. So let's get started.

Narrator: Matt pulled off his shorts revealing a pair of tight Speedo underwear. Jenny slipped it off and began performing that pushing hump that Mark taught her, and squeezed Matt's *pienis*. As this went on, a cop car pulled up and stopped next to the convertible. He peered into the back seat.

Cop: I don't suppose your parents know what's going on.
Matt: Actually officer, our parents our out of town.
Cop: Then it would seem that you to shouldn't be engaged in such an activity. Don't let me find you here again.
Jenny: That drives me so fucking crazy. Once, I was doing it with this one guy. The cop wouldn't go away so eventually I gave it to the cop and then he finally left. (Jenny lights a cigarette.)
Matt: Cool. So, do you want to do this again sometime? It was, uh, satisfying.
Jenny: Maybe for you.

And that's the end. After forty pages of endless humping incredibly and frenching wildly, those are the last two lines: He says, "It was satisfying," and she says, "Maybe for you"—which I think is such a bizarrely on-target predictor of the way that actual sex would really unfold for me almost eight years later, when I finally got humped for real in a wide variety of college dorm rooms.

CHANEL INC.
new york, 10019

Dear Models,
    As you all know. My new coll
And Im telling you be
you wish to investigat
you dont have to read.
1 male(elegant)model. If
at 11:00 AM we will be ta
see me. Thank you.

THE CHANEL MEMOS
Cheryl Calegari

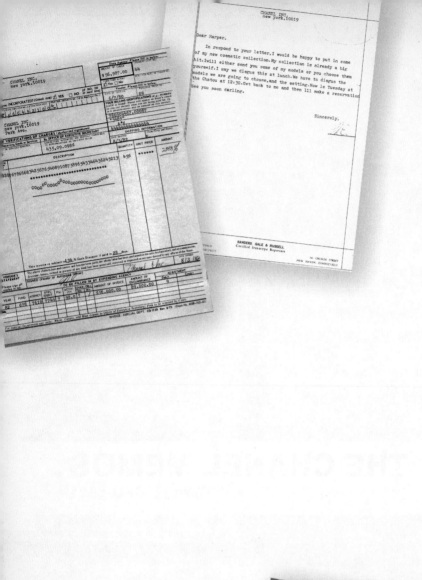

CHANEL INC
new york,10019

Dear Harper,

In respond to your letter,I would be happy to put in come of my new cosmetic collection.My collection is already a big hit.Iwill either send you some of my models or you choose them yourself.I say we disgus this at lunch.We have to disgus the models we are going to choose,and the setting.How is Tuesday at the Chatou at 12:30.Get back to me and then Ill make a reservation See you soon darling.

Sincerely,

SANDERS GALE & RUSSELL
Certified Stenotype Reporters

16 CHURCH STREET
NEW HAVEN, CONNECTICUT

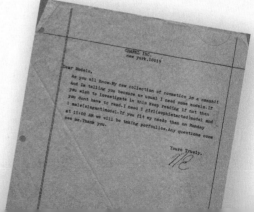

CHANEL INC.
new york,10019

Dear Models,

As you all know.My new collection of cosmetics is a smash!! And Im telling you because as usual I need some models.If you wish to investigate in this keep reading if not then you dont have to read.I need 1 girl(sophisticated)model and 1 male(elegant)model.If you fit my needs then on Monday at 11:00 AM we will be taking portfoilios.Any questions come see me.Thank you.

Yours truely,

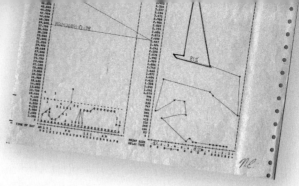

My mother recently found these letters while cleaning out the many stored boxes I keep in her basement. While most nine-year-olds used to play kickball outside on hot summer nights, I was running Chanel Inc.

I was always obsessed with the Chanel No. 9 and Alexis Carrington. My fictitious persona was Natasha, a young Russian immigrant who took New York City by storm!

I used to steal boxes of paper from my mom, type out my own personalized letterhead, and make up flow charts and graphs on my dad's computer printouts and old tax returns. Then I'd sit at the typewriter for hours and conduct "important business," using words that could have only come from watching *Dynasty*.

Dear Mr. Ontario,

Chanel Inc. has come out with a new collection of cosmetics. I would like to know if you want to invest in my collection. As always you would get 10% of the estimated shares. Last year you know my Chanel Emulsion No. 1 Skin Equilibrium Formula was an estimated $25,000 success. And like always you did get your 10%. Well I just wanted to inform you on my new collection. If you conciter please inform me before August 15, 1979. Thank you.

Yours Truely,

Natasha

Dear Models,

As you all know, my new collection of cosmetics is a smash!! And I'm telling you because as usual I need some models. If you wish to investigate in this keep reading. If not, then you don't have to read. I need 1 girl sophistacted model and 1 male elegant model. If you fit my needs then on Monday at 11:00am we will be taking porfolios. Any questions come see me. Thank you.

Yours Truely,

Natasha

Dear Harper,

In respond to your letter, I would be happy to put in some of my new cosmetics collection. My collection is already a big hit. I will either send you some of my models or you choose them yourself. I say we disgus this at lunch. We have to disgus the models we are going to choose and the setting. How is Tuesday at the Chatou at 12:30? Get back to me and then I'll make a reservation. See you soon darling.

Sincerely,

Natasha

Dear Pierre,

Your new collection is devine. I love what you are doing and wish you all the best. It's been 2 years now and I think we should merge. Pierre Cardin is a smash and so is my new cosmetic collection. Everyone is talking about it. Let's have dinner at the Chatou and we can disgus the details. You can make the reservation or I can make the reservation. Let me know and I will have the lawyers draw up the contracts immediately.

Yours Truely,

Natasha

Dear Anne,

When did you get back from the Alpes? Dominic and I had such a great vacation with you and Mr. Klein. Let's go skiing again soon. I want you to know that my new cosmetic collection is a hit. My Chanel No. 5 and Chanel No. 5 Loose Body Powder is taking the world by storm. I would like you to see it and buy a stake in the company. I also have great models that you should use for the new commercial. Television is the future and I think we can do this. Let's meet tomorrow in the boardroom and meet. I know we can be a hit together!

Yours Truley,

Natasha

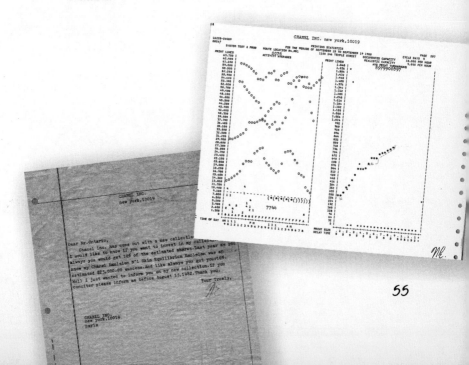

DON'T FEED THE FAT KID

Qraig de Groot

The following is an essay I wrote in seventh grade that I called "de Groot the Great." During my junior high years I was known as "the fat kid." I knew very well that I was fat, but I never really understood why. Perhaps what I wrote will give you a clue as to *why* I was so big.

My name is Qraig de Groot. My first name is Scottish and means a person who lives in a crag region. My last name is Dutch. My last name is also split into two parts "de" and "Groot." Dutch names are usually like that.

I was born on February 1, 1971 at 8:05am and I weighed 6 pounds 8 ounces. I was born in the sign of Aquarius. A lot of my friends from elementary school call me Keggie. They started calling me that last year when my 6th grade teacher slipped and said *"Keg, get your paper."* Then from then on they have been calling me that.

I am 5 feet 4 inches tall. My hair color is dirty blonde. My eyes are a bluish shade. I would rather not tell you my weight. I like to wear all kind of clothes, especially jeans. I am in pretty good health. I have no allergies or illnesses. I only really get colds, stomachaches, earaches . . . you know stuff like that. I fall a lot and I hit my knees and elbows a lot on stuff like cabinets, trees, ground, furniture, etc. . . .

If you went into my room you would know I am not very coordinated. I like to leave things lying around because I am too lazy to put them away after I take it out.

I am not very athletic. I do not play many sports. All I do is bowl. I like to watch games on TV like football, baseball, tennis and bowling. My favorite football team is the Giants even though they cannot play football at all! I do not have a favorite baseball or tennis player. I have a favorite bowler, Anthony something; I don't know his last name.

I have a lot of favorite things. One thing I like the most is music. My favorite kind of music is rock. I really do not have a favorite group. I have a lot of favorite songs. Some are "Cum on Feel the Noize" by Quiet Riot, "Karma Chameleon" by Culture Club and "Love is a Battlefield" by Pat Benatar.

There are many movies and TV shows I like. My favorite kind of movies is science fiction like *Star Wars*, *Empire Strikes Back* and *Return of the Jedi*. A lot of TV shows I like are comedies. I like *Knight Rider*, *Fame*, *The Facts of Life*, *Family Ties* and *Whiz Kids*. There are not any actors I like, but there are a couple of actresses I like. They are Nancy McKeon who plays Jo on *The Facts of Life* and Erica Gimpel who plays Coco Hernandez on *Fame*.

I have a few hobbies. One is collecting stamps, which I like the most. I also like watching TV. I like reading science fiction and horror books. I like to program computers. There is only one thing I like more than any other of my hobbies—spending money. Not my money but other people's money!!

Another thing I really like is food.

I like Italian food like linguini and white clam sauce,

spaghetti and meatballs, fettuccini and cheese raviolis. I also like southern fried chicken and macaroni and cheese.

Another category of food I like is seafood. The most favorite seafood I like is clams dipped in butter, stuffed clams, stuffed flounder, fried shrimp, fried fish sandwiches, fried clams and fried flounder.

I also very much like junk food.

ADULT ME SAYS

I actually loved food so much as a kid that I even wrote a poem about one of my favorite delicacies. The following poem is simply titled "Fried Chicken."

"Fried Chicken"
>   Fried Chicken
>   Golden Brown coating
>   Crisp to touch
>   Steam rising—aroma carried swiftly to nose
>   Coating breaks away when bitten
>   Teeth sink into tender juicy white chicken meat
>   Whets my appetite
>   Meat tears neatly from bone
>   What a taste.

PIONEER PRAYERS

Hayley Downs

In 1988, when I was fifteen years old, I fell suddenly and madly in love . . . with Jesus. I started demanding that my parents—who were ambivalent about religion—drive me to a very strict Southern Baptist church five days a week for services, choir, youth group, potluck dinners, and optional Bible studies. I had myself baptized in front of the congregation and asked that a party be thrown in my honor after the ceremony.

Eventually I graduated to an "advanced" sleepaway Christian youth camp called Pioneer Plunge in the North Carolina mountains, where we lived as nineteenth-century homesteaders for two weeks.

I had always been a slightly eccentric and very dramatic kid, and I often felt misunderstood in the rural central-Florida town where I grew up. As a born-again, I finally had something in common with other people, and my natural intensity was welcomed and even applauded in this comfortable new world of passionate devotion.

August 1

We left home shortly after 6:00 PM. The van is crowded and I feel it will be a long ride. We're stopping in Columbia, South Carolina tonight and then it's off to Pioneer Plunge. I must admit, I'm afraid of what's before me and nervous about how well I'll fare. I expressed my qualms to Clay and he gave me a good bit of advice in the form of Philippians 4:13.

August 2

I didn't know what rustic meant until I got to Pioneer Plunge. The main building serves as a kitchen and a meeting room. The toilet facilities are in the form of an outhouse. The show is a mountain stream and sources of light are fires and flashlights. We have a pig, Leroy, that we will slaughter and a goat named Billie. Later on we have a solo, which is two days in the mountains, alone, with no food.

I must admit I'm having second thoughts about my "Plunge." I'm afraid of the dark. After I crawl into my sleeping bag I'll talk with God about it.

August 3

It's the early evening and I feel wonderful! I was in Kitchen Crew today. We woke up early and sang "rise and shine" to the sleeping campers. I made the biscuits. After breakfast was Bible study. After that we played challenge games that were designed to bring us closer together in the body of Christ. Nobody is any better than anyone here. We're all equals.

Question: if it was illegal to be a Christian, would I be convicted by my actions?

August 4

Had a great quiet time today. I chose a beautiful spot—I'll return there tomorrow. I laid on my back and green leaves covered me overhead. The morning light shone through and I rested my head on my Bible as I prayed. I talked with God for ever so long. We discussed everything and he helped me understand some things in his divine way.

Pancakes are for breakfast! See you later!

Later in the day . . .

Today I was on cabin building [duty]. We "chinked." This is the method of placing wire mesh over insulation and placing concrete over that. I'm tired, my hands are cut and my fingernails are dirty but I feel wonderful! I'm blissfully exhausted! Tonight we hung out in the main cabin talking and roasting marshmallows. It feels good to be close. I think Marilyn and Logan are getting together.

I wonder . . . is Pioneer Plunge the right environment?

August 5

The prayer meeting was interesting. We talked about our Bible reading and somehow became engrossed in a heated discussion about religion and whether or not different religions receive eternal life. It was strange to see the leaders so extremely serious and almost . . . hostile. I believe that it's not our place to question, even if we're educated. Maybe that's my opinion because I'm ignorant about such things but I can't help thinking that my Lord didn't intend for us to try and interpret his methods. But then again, questioning whether or not to question is still questioning.

August 6

My crew was on wood chopping today. I feel I worked hard but not as hard as I could have. Why is it that I love God so much but I have such a hard time spending time with him? My quiet time even suffered today. I sometimes have such trouble talking to Jesus. Why? Why? Why? He loves me so much and I love him. I just don't get it.

August 7

Kitchen crew today! French toast and bacon and Romans 12!

Later in the day . . .

I'm so tired and my feet hurt. I heard through the grapevine that our solo is on Tuesday. Even though I'll be frightened in the dark I'll enjoy the time to spend with God—fasting. Tonight we're having chili and I hate chili. I conflicted with Christine today. I miss God and I think he misses me. See you later!

August 8

It is almost evening and I'm on the first day of my solo. The rain is coming down and it's hard to write. I've discovered holes in my tarp and my sleeping bag has failed to be waterproof. So I'm sitting on a rock away from my camp sight trying to shield myself from the rain.

I did a foolish, foolish thing today. Instead of staying awake and praying like I was supposed to do, I took a nap. I couldn't help it and now the consequences will be a lack of sleep tonight—I'm going to be terrified. It's getting dark so I'll write again tomorrow.

Good night!

August 9

This is the second day of my solo. Last night was the best and worst night of my whole life. It started to get dark and I crawled into my sleeping bag and closed my eyes. I finally got to sleep, but then all of a sudden I woke up and it was pitch black. I prayed for God to have mercy on me. Tears of frustration fell from my eyes. "Why?" I asked. "Why, why, why?" I must have fallen asleep because the next time I woke up it was morning. Small bugs were buzzing around my face and my hands were bitten and scratched.

Through all of it I did it for the Lord and he was with me. He laid beside me and gently put me to sleep. He shooed away the snakes and bandits. Without his divine mercy, I know I would have died. Thank you dear Jesus!

August 10

The Day the Lights Went Out in Leroy

It was an early day for all of us. We dressed and ate a light breakfast—calm. We walked down to the pen. All of us together, a body of Christ. Water was boiling in a big kettle and Leroy was in his pigpen. A group of us went in to get him. We chased him, grabbed him by the legs and wheelbarrowed him from his home.

I watch through the film of a nightmare. Two held him from behind and Tom, my gentle friend, took a sledgehammer and brought it down on my friend Leroy's head. Screams, terrible, terrible screams. Over and over Tom came down on his skull.

Antley said, "Suzanne now! Quick!" Suzanne moved in and cut Leroy's throat.

From behind my tears I looked on Tom. Sledgehammer in hand he kneeled, gazing at the lifeless Leroy.

Boiling water was poured over Leroy and then knives were used to strip off all of his hair. Other things, tribal rituals were performed on Leroy. He was strung up, gutted, quartered and barbequed.

For the rest of my life I'll remember hugging Tom in his shock. For the rest of my life I'll see him swing the hammer and hear Leroy's final cry.

Think back, thousands of years. "You, you and you, catch the beast." Peels of laughter sounded and then, silence. Then there was shock. The comparison was as clear to me as Leroy's lifeless eyes.

Thank you Jesus for Pioneer Plunge.

Last Day

I'm on the bus now going home. The tears have finally dried on my swollen face. I feel empty. I have experienced something new and extraordinary at Pioneer Plunge. Something that I feel everyone should know. The written word is a nice way to get the word out. Maybe, just maybe, after I'm dead, someone will find this journal and feel just a fraction of what I have felt these past two incredible weeks.

So Long Utopia—Hello High School!

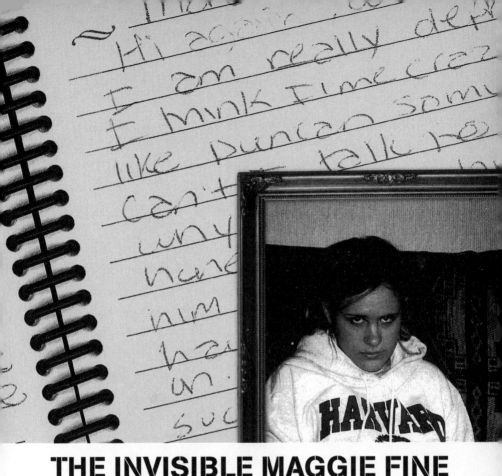

THE INVISIBLE MAGGIE FINE

Maggie Fine

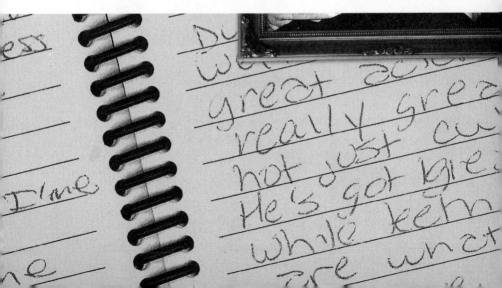

As a kid, I spent endless hours dreaming about what it might be like to have the power of invisibility. But as a teenager, I spent every second wondering what it would be like just to be *noticed*.

I was becoming a woman. I was tired of being the Invisible Maggie Fine. And I desperately wanted someone, anyone, to remember me.

March 23, 1995

Well today was yet another day. I started my period, I haven't had it in five months, and I was both relieved and disgusted. Since I've had my period so seldom I haven't used a tampon since I fainted last year. I'm just sure I have toxic shock syndrome. Of course, that's just the way my life goes. I can't do it, it won't fit. Maybe something's wrong with me.

Did I tell you that Kate has a new boyfriend? Yeah, she's getting all weird now. Figures. She is a temporary person anyway, I know she'll have no lasting effect on my life. I guess I'm jealous I mean I'm happy for her but why don't I have a boyfriend? I guess I'm afraid of boys. What are you supposed to say to them? I must be depressed! Maybe I should kill myself and get it over with. Then again I could never be an actress if that happened.

Okay this is it. I'm making a cut off point, if I'm not a successful actress by the age of 28 I'm jumping off the Brooklyn Bridge on August 10, 2009. Hasn't that already been done? Maybe I should jump off Hoover Damn instead, that's more original, plus my grandfather helped build it so it would make a better story. Too bad I wouldn't enjoy it because I'd be dead, but maybe they'd make a TV movie of my life.

I wonder if all the dead movie stars are proud of their lives. I'm sure Marilyn is very happy she's a legend. I must stop talking like this. I hate having suicidal thoughts. I wish I were more carefree and happy. Everyone likes those kinds of people.

I wish I were a lot of things. I can't spend my whole life wishing, I must go out and fight for what I want. I wish I had a boyfriend. NO!!!!!!!! I'm going to *get* a boyfriend, starting tomorrow I will get myself a guy. The only problem is, which guy?

I wish it was Matt Bernstein or Duncan Meckeljohn, I want a guy like that. I want to be sexy and seductive and funny. How do I do that?

1. Dress Nice, take a shower

2. Make eye contact and smile

3. Be cold and icy also

4. RELAX

That should be my personal motto. Let's see, tomorrow I will deliberately be sexy and smile and be a leader. I am a Leo. That's my job. What's my problem? This stuff should come naturally to me. I know I'm funny, I have nice teeth, but I don't think I'm very sexy. One isn't born sexy, they have to make themselves be sexy. I have to walk more friendly; I should swing my arms more and smile. I'm going to rent *Pretty Woman* and watch Julia Roberts. I am going to make the guys want me.

Pretend Conversation when I see Duncan tomorrow.

Maggie: (Smile) Hey surfer boy

Duncan: Hey Mags how's it hangin?

Maggie: Not so bad if I may say so myself. How's life treating Mr. Stud?

Duncan: What? Oh, pretty good.

Maggie: Well good. I'll see ya later Duncan.

(Smile and walk opposite direction without looking back)

Damnit!!!!!!!! I wish I could do this. We'll see. I will do something like this I swear.

April 1, 1995

Right now I feel like a car on the edge of a cliff, I could either fall into a canyon full of sorrow and unhappiness or push full blast on the accelerator towards happiness and stardom. I applied to the American Academy of Dramatic Arts for teens in New York City but I haven't received an acceptance letter yet. What if I don't get in? Oh god this agony is killing me. If I don't get in I am going to become psychotically depressed. I can feel the darkness overtaking me as I write.

I just finished this amazing book called *The Bell Jar* by Sylvia Plath. She and I are very similar, as was reading the book I actually felt her speak through me. She stuck her head in the oven. I think that's sort of gross, but then again if you must go she certainly made a grand exit.

Besides feeling depressed I am in love with this guy named Duncan Meckeljohn. He's so cute and I'm so ugly. It's just so tragic. Not only that but because I'm so fucking shy around guys I can't say a word when I'm around him so he thinks I have a boring personality. I don't! Not at all! At least I hope not. Maybe I *am* boring. Oh well. I should stop fantasizing anyway I'll probably never get a guy as long as I live, they all probably think I'm boring and ugly and have no personality. My parents probably think I'm a lesbian because I'm 14 and I don't have a boyfriend yet.

Heck, I haven't even kissed a guy yet, how sick is that? You must never repeat this information to anyone, do you understand? I never have kissed a guy because let's face it, I am UGLY. I've looked in the mirror. I know an ugly person when I see one. I'm ugly. Besides no boys think I'm pretty and they're the only ones that count anyways. I wish I looked like my best friend Kate. She's pretty. Every boy likes her.

I want to be an actress more than anything in the world, even more than I want a boyfriend. When I'm on stage it's the only time I'm completely happy because then I'm not stupid Maggie Fine anymore. I'm someone else. Maybe someday I'll get to play the part of Kate.

Well its 9:30, I better get my beauty rest, even though I'm ugly.

April 5, 1995

Hi again, right now I am really depressed. I think I'm crazy I like Duncan so much. Why can't I talk to him, WHY!!!!!!???????????? I love him I honestly do, well not love him I mustn't be overdramatic but I do have a severe heart-wrenching crush on him. I've never had such a big crush on a guy and we both know I've liked a lot of guys. Why do I like Duncan? I don't know. Well . . .

1. He's a great actor
2. He has a sharp jaw line
3. Pearly white teeth (a male must have this to meet my approval)

I wish I could forget about him for 30 seconds. I hope I do. I hope my mom's flu gets better, I hope Duncan likes me, I hope my dog doesn't miss me too much when I go see my dad, I hope my family stays healthy, I hope the shopping center sells, I hope I'm a movie star when I grow up, I hope Brad Pitt marries me, I hope Duncan likes me, I hope I get an "A" in Biology, I hope my dad doesn't yell at me, I hope I get good presents this Christmas, I hope this plane doesn't crash, I hope there's peace on earth and I hope Duncan likes me.

April 15, 1995

Well, the time has come. It's 10:05 and tonight's a school night. I wish it wasn't. I'm excited to see Duncan and yet I know deep down nothing will happen. I can see it all before my eyes.

Tomorrow I will go to school. I will go through all my classes. I will pass him on the way from English to Biology between 3rd and 4th period and I will glance in his direction but he will not be looking at me. He will be playing hackey sack. I love his hackey sack. He's really good at it. Then I will see him when I get back from lunch sitting outside with his Art class before they go inside. Again, I will glance his way but there is only a 65% chance he will look my way. If I'm with Kate he will look at her. Then at three o'clock as the end of the day approaches I will descend the stairs and he will be playing hackey sack again in the parking lot. I will linger in the parking lot and pretend I am talking to someone else until he walks to his light blue Honda Civic and I will cross paths with him on the way to my car. That is the only moment we will have together. That moment is my one shot for happiness.

I am so tired of fantasizing about all the conversations we could have and then fucking it up in real life. I wish I were as good in real life as I am in fake life.

April 24, 1995

It is now 11:13 pm on Friday night and I just got back from the movie *Pulp Fiction*, it is a movie about dirt bag people living their dirt bag lives. It was *brilliant*. There's this girl in it named Mia Wallace and I'm going to be just like her when I grow up. Except that she's a drug addict but other than that she is soooooooooooooooooo cool.

I have this problem. All week nothing happened with Duncan except a few word exchanges:

Duncan: Hey Mags
Me: Hey Duncan (I get clammed up, start shaking and walk away)

Stupid!!!!
Tomorrow night there is this BASH that he will be at and I want to go but I made plans to sleep at Mary's. To lie or not to

lie, that is the question. Or shall I say to go or not to go THAT is the question. I mean what if I go to the Bash and nothing interesting happens and I lie to Mary and tell her I can't make it and then she hates me the rest of my life. Or should I go to Mary's and have a bad attitude because I'm not at the BASH? Or what if I lie to Mary and go to the BASH and see Duncan and we talk and he asks me out and Mary never finds out I lied and I live happily ever after. Oh God, I feel I should grasp this opportunity to go to the BASH. I mean what if Option Three really came true? Wouldn't that be great? Oh God I'll just go to sleep and worry about it in the morning. I am sure I'll have an ulcer by the age of 20. Well it's 11:24 pm. Sleep awaits.

TTFN,

Mags

May 3, 1995

I am so sorry I haven't written in so long, I've just been too busy. I went out to dinner with Melissa (the most popular girl in my class) last week and it was really fun. I mean I finally felt like YES I'm with someone popular for a change. Not that my friends are nerds, but listen to this. In one night we went out to dinner, went to Melissa's boyfriend Damien's house (who is 21) went downtown, went to pick up Grace, went to Café Oasis, went back to Damien's, went back downtown, went back to her house, played pool, watched *Adventures in Babysitting*, made pancakes and went to bed. I mean THAT'S LIVING!!!!!!!!!! It is becoming clear to me that I am destined for life in the fast lane.

But you want to know what? I went to school on Monday

thinking I'd made a new great popular friend . . . . NOT. She barely said two words to me.. Oh well I guess that's life.

Duncan talked to me this week. I don't really know what he said but he still talked to me—not that I won an Academy Award or anything but I guess that's cool. You know what else? I'm starting to get higher self-esteem.

May 26, 1995

Oh Fuck. Oh Shit. So I got the lead in the musical *Fame* this summer which is totally rad. But get this. Oh God I have the biggest knot in my stomach. I just found out Randy is the guy working opposite me in *Fame*. He's the first guy I'll ever kiss. Why????? He's so weird, he has huge pimples and he smells. I feel sick. I think I'm going to cry I have tears running down my face.

On top of kissing someone disgusting, I have to kiss someone for the first time in front of a huge group of people. What if I can't do it? I mean maybe there's some secret way to do it that no one tells you. I wish Duncan were in the play with me. I guess I'll just pretend Randy is Duncan.

You know what? I bet this is test to see how good of an actress I am. If I can't kiss Randy I will never be an actress, I must be strong.

I'm still totally disgusted.

May 30, 1995

I am writing now. This may quite possibly the last time I write in you again. Not because I don't love you but because I may decide to not wake up tomorrow morning. Guess what?

I just found out Kate is going to be in summer P.E with Duncan. Do you know what this means? HE IS GOING TO LIKE HER!!!!! I could DIE.

I WANT DUNCAN. I DESERVE DUNCAN, He is MY guy, WE ARE MADE FOR EACH OTHER!!!!! I LOVE DUNCAN. I want him, not next year, not never, NOW!!!!!!!!!!!!!!!!!!!!!!!!!!! !!!!!!!! I want him so bad I can taste it. I DESERVE HIM. I am truly LOSING IT. OH please if someone is out there MAKE DUNCAN COME INTO MY LIFE. I have waited long enough. DO NOT DISAPPOINT ME!!!!!

June 8, 1995

Oh my Fucking God. Guess what I did tonight? I CALLED DUNCAN. I just did it!

Real life phone conversation between me and Duncan:

Me: Hello, is Duncan there?

Duncan: Speaking.

Me: Hey Duncan, it's Maggie.

Duncan: Who?

Me: It's Maggie, Maggie Fine, the girl in your third period drama class.

Duncan: Oh right. What's up?

Me: Ummmmmm, just wanted to say hi I guess.

Duncan: Hi.

Me: Yeah, so do you want to do something sometime?

Duncan: Well this isn't a great week for me to tell you the truth. My brother is in town, but maybe some other time. I'll tell you what, let me get back to you.

Me: Of course, I mean yeah. Well have a good night, see you tomorrow I guess.

Duncan: Yeah, see you.

(abrupt hang up)

ADULT ME SAYS

This conversation was the first time I actually "spoke" with Duncan, and it's the last time I ever wrote about him. I'm sure I saw him a few times after that, but in all honesty I can't even tell you what he looked like.

Yes, I wanted to be remembered. But the truth of the matter is that the *only* thing I remember is that I hung up the phone that night not quite sure why I'd dialed his number in the first place.

Bolls! THE Judge told me that he w
going to mark me down for not identi
what sample three was infested with
I WAS SHOCKED,
it wasn't the
as it? he sa
ton Boll worm.
EY ARE THE S
ME FUCKING
thats when
him it was
erent name.

THE COTTON CLUB
Lori Fowler

corn ear worm. on corn
ot back what if
Grew across the
from the corn and
orms crossed the
? THEY what wo
called?!?

I grew up in a small town called Porterville. It's in between Fresno and Bakersfield, also known as the armpit of California. Growing up there I had few choices to fit in. I wasn't athletic enough for the track team or popular enough to be a cheerleader, and you don't want to hear me sing.

So I followed the family tradition and became a proud member of the Cotton Judging Team. The cotton judging team is part of FFA, or Future Farmers of America.

So consider this: I *judged* cotton and then was *judged* on how well I *judged* cotton. I was like Tom Cruise in *Top Gun*—I was really good at what I did, but my methods scared those in charge. They feared me. Nobody tells me how to judge cotton. *Nobody*.

The following is from my freshman year of high school.

August 15th, 1997

So I joined the cotton judging team, and well I'm going to judge it. I mean after all, it is the fabric of our lives. My friends think I'm a dork, and well maybe I am, but I look at it this way. I am participating in high school, not just being a spectator.

August 21st, 1997

Ok, I felt like a complete idiot today. We took a practice test, and I got in an argument over the colors of cotton. The question read something like: What colors of cotton grow in the United States?

A. Cream

B. Brown

C. Blue

D. White or

E. none of the above.

I knew the obvious answer was white. But being the dumb ass that I am I chose E, because no one answer by itself was right, and being that it was an "easy" question I was the only one who got it "wrong." He asked me what I chose and I told him "E" and then he asked my why, and I told him that no one answer was right on its own. I then proceeded to tell him that some of the cotton that grows out on Ave. 280 is kinda of a cream color, and that my Uncle Coy grows brown cotton by the hundred acre in Missouri.

Then he asked where do they grow blue cotton? I told him that a couple universities including Fresno State, had some genetically altered cotton. I then proceeded to put my foot in my mouth and say that they grow white cotton the most, and is also the most desirable cotton at this time. I think this pissed him off. He then told me that he would like to see me after practice was over. I smiled and sat down. I was on a high, and didn't really catch the rest of what happened. Practice ended, and I proceeded to get chewed out for being a smart ass.

I knew I was right. I let him say his piece, but if there is a question on there like that then I will make a stink again!

September 1st, 1997

I have my first actual competition this weekend. I'm a bit nervous, and I have to get my uniform together. I have to find a black skirt that goes to my knees, and black dress shoes that have no heel. I just got my FFA jacket and scarf in the mail yesterday. I really like the jacket. On the front it has my name on it, and on the back it has the national FFA Emblem. I can't wait till I get my green-hand pin. I saw my uncle's FFA jacket, and he has all kinds of pins, and medals. I guess we get pins for every conference we attend, and any accomplishment we make. It's kinda like the varsity jacket of farming. I have lettered in farming. Wonderful.

September 3rd, 1997

Ok, we competed regionally today, and its nothing like I expected. These kids are really serious about the cotton, and I'm way out of my league. They come in and are like cotton judging machines. I hung out with Travis, as he is a sophomore, and already knows the ropes. He explained that you don't talk to people from other schools until the judging is over. He also told me to put my pre-notes in the inside pocket, so that when I'm taking notes, my terms aren't out for everyone to see. He also told me that you do not under any circumstances ask questions to another person judging.

We all look like dorks, and I think its totally unfair that the guys get to wear pants. I wish I could wear pants. I wonder if them making women wear skirts is suppressing us in the organization. I guess I should be thankful they let me in at all, there was a time that girls were not even allowed to be in FFA. I wonder what went through their minds when they made this decision.

"Well if girls want to farm then they will do it in skirts!" I think it's an unreasonable request. How would they feel if we made them farm in skirts? Boys suck.

On a side note, our team won second place, and that was pretty cool. We got a plaque for the school, and Travis got high individual for Lint. That boy knows his stuff apparently.

September 6

We had a recap and got our judges' comments back. I talk too fast. That was said on every judge's sheet—that I talk too fast. Well I don't think I talk too fast, okay maybe if I'm nervous which I admit I was for Plants since it was my first official set of reasons, and then for Bolls because I couldn't decide what was my top pick. The top pair was so close, and I was sure I was missing something. Okay, so I give my reasons a little on the fast side. I'm just tryin' not to waste their time, I mean after all they are listening to a hundred set of reasons, and any way I can help I thought would be greatly appreciated. Well I was wrong.

Mr. Catano wants me to practice talking slow, so I got home, and my mom asked me how my day was, and I told her "it was fine, thanks for asking" really slowly, and then she yelled at me for being a smartass. I can't win.

September 9th, 1997

I got into an argument with a judge last night when I was giving reasons for bolls. The judge told me he was going to mark me down for not identifying correctly what sample three was infested with. I was shocked, and asked him if it wasn't the corn earworm what was it? He said that it was cotton bollworm. WHAT THE FUCK? They are the same thing. Same fucking worm. Well that's when I lost it. I told him that it was the same thing, just a different name.

He told me that when its on cotton it's referred to as cotton bollworm, and when it's on corn it's a corn earworm. I shot back what if the cotton grew across the street from corn, and the worms crossed the street? Then what would they be called? He told me to calm down. Did I? Nope I continued, that it doesn't matter what you call it, IT still ate the fucking sample (except I didn't say "fucking", I didn't think it would be appropriate.) I then asked him that if we had one of the worms, and it was found in the middle of the road, between the corn and the cotton, what then would it be called? Would a corn earworm by any other name still eat cotton? I walked out, and was disqualified from the boll competition.

September 16th, 1997

I don't understand why we are practicing five days a week. I have a life outside of cotton. I have homework and stuff to do. I don't think they expect us to do anything except eat, breath, and live cotton. I am going to start wearing anything but cotton. I know so much more about cotton than I ever thought I would, and apparently there is a lot more to learn. I don't care if the fibers are hollow stands of cellulose, or that cotton is related to okra. Who gives a shit?

September 20th, 1997

We have our green-hand banquet coming up, and I'm excited about it, all except getting my hand dyed. We have to stick our hand in this goopy stuff that dyes our hands up to our elbow green. I think this is a form of hazing, and I thought that was illegal. It also couldn't happen at a better time, we have a meet the next day, and I have to go with my hand green. Everyone will know I'm a freshman. I asked Mr. Catano if I could skip that part, and he told me no. I told him that I didn't think a green-hand went well with the FFA uniform, and he told me that everyone will understand, as they all have done it at one time or another, and tradition this and tradition that. And I stopped listening.

Ok, so I had to go to the meet with a bright green hand. I tried everything to get it off. It doesn't wash off, and apparently they have spent several years perfecting the recipe, so that it *can't* be washed off. I tried dish soap, mechanics hand cleaner, lye, and vinegar. The only thing I didn't try is gasoline, because my mom wouldn't let me. I went in to shake the judges hands, and they couldn't help but laugh, but I think I got sympathy points for it.

I placed second in plants, and third in seeds. I'll take whatever I can get.

October 3rd, 1997

We had another meet yesterday. The only one who didn't place was Tiffany. Hmm, let's see if she gets singled out in practice tomorrow. She should. She is just doing this to meet guys. Bitch.

October 10, 1997
Okay, so I'm thinking about quitting this whole cotton-judging thing. I can't stand our coach. He picks on me, I swear. He thinks I don't know what I'm doing, which is true, but he doesn't need to call me on it. As long as I can make people believe that I know what I'm talking about, that's what matters, and at the last contest I got above 40 in all my sets of reasons, so what is he worrying about? I think he is just being a hard ass. I don't know if I can take his shit anymore.

Fuck him. Fuck Cotton.

My favorite class

My favorite class is
I like it beca
informative. We
things to help k
For example
what food d
eating too many
could give
trol. We

I HAVE A DREAM
Jon Friedman

I'm getting pussy
my nootchie hole. My
teacher says that when
we should wear a
not getting aids.
die from aids but
that if

These are all journal entries that I wrote as school assignments at the ages of ten, twelve, and fourteen. The school system I was raised in was very big on the students' keeping journals in English class.

When reading through these old entries, it is very clear that the minimum requirement per assignment was at least one page in length. All of my entries end somewhat abruptly or hurry to finish up as soon as I reach the one-page qualification.

I can remember being sincere when writing these entries. I was an innocent, quiet, good boy who wanted to please those around me.

Things I Dream About

Things I dream about is that there are no more drugs. In my dream this boy was about to take drugs. When he was just about to sniff it, it disappeared. Then I was going to read the newspaper and it said, "Peace to the World." I went to tell everybody. They were excited. I saw something else that said everybody will live a longer and healthier life. They did something to the air.

My Dream Girl

My dream girl is (of course) a girl who should really understand me and love me for what I am. I would hope they understand my feelings and want to be with me as often as they can. We would call each other and write notes to each other. I would also like her to be good looking, have a good sense of humor, and be nice to other people.

Love is

Love is when you really care about someone or something. You should really worry about it. If you do then you know that you truly love it when you worry! If you want an example of love take my parents. I know that they really love me. They would do anything for me but they won't spoil me at all. My parents truly love me.

Getting Left Back

I think getting left back is fair. If kids don't do the work in 7th grade they should stay back in the 7th grade until they do the work that they are supposed to do. I told this kid that he was going to get left back because his grades were really low and he acted like he didn't even care. I couldn't believe it. I disagree with summer school. Left back is enough.

Cartoon

If I could be a cartoon character I would be the very funny Bugs Bunny from the Looney Tunes. I like Bugs because he makes lots of jokes and is very smart when trouble arrives. I wouldn't like to be Daffy Duck because he always falls for Bugs Bunny's tricks. He also spits wherever he goes, which doesn't attract women.

If I Were Born a Girl

If I were born a girl I think my life would be pretty much the opposite. I wouldn't like girls, I would like guys. I wouldn't like sports as much or collect baseball cards as much. I wouldn't probably live in the same home.

The Best Gift I Can Give

The best gift that I think I can give someone is love and happiness. I love to make people happy and laugh. It gives people a good feeling when people laugh when they say something funny. And it makes the people who are laughing in a good mood. If they were in a bad mood they wouldn't be laughing.

War Journal

My feelings on the war are very sad. I don't think people should die over oil. I'd much rather have the high price or no oil at all then have a death of a loved one. We also must defend our country. There may be a draft and many of my relatives or even me and my own brother could be drafted in the future. On the other hand Saddam Hussein is said to be the next Hitler and he must be stopped. If he can take over Kuwait so easily then he will work his way up and start taking over other countries. He has gotten his people to worship him just as Hitler did. So you can see my feelings on the war are mixed. I am mainly worried about any terrorist acts, and deaths of innocent people.

Things That Annoy Me

Some things in life really annoy me. For example, in the summer time there are bugs that fly up my nose, in my ears, and in my eyes. This to me is very annoying. Another annoyance in my life is when I am trying to sleep and my neighbors are up bright and early mowing the lawn or washing the car.

Even though I love my family at times they can be very annoying. My brother can be annoying especially when I am in a bad mood. My parents can get annoying by repeatively asking or telling me to do something for example, take out the garbage, do the dishes, please do the laundry.

ADULT ME SAYS

This last entry was written by my older artist brother in *my* handwriting. Unaware, I submitted my journal for school with his entry in it.

Favorite Class

My Favorite class is Health. I like it because it is very informative. We learn useful things to help keep us healthy. For example when we learned about food I was taught that having too many eggs and cheese could give me a high cholesterol. We learn good things about everyday life. Another example of this is for when I'm getting pussy from my hootchie hole. My health teacher says that when we bone we should wear a condom for not getting AIDS. You could die from AIDS but I think that if you don't fuck around you could be ok. Also in Health sometimes we watch movies with tits. I like Health because it is fun and sleazy.

There was no specific reaction or discipline made by my teacher as a result of this entry. I did, however, receive a low grade, with only a note saying, "These seem rushed." Or it is possible that, like me, she was too rushed and did not read any of these entries but only counted the pages?

I confronted my brother about the entry; that resulted in a huge laugh between him and me. When he wrote it, he thought that I had *already* turned it in and got it back.

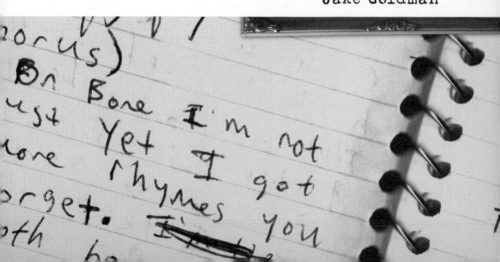

PUMPMASTER AND SMOOTH BOYZ

Jake Goldman

I used to rap. I was 14, just about 6 feet tall, 120 pounds, and very white. I lived across the street from a farm, so my knowledge of rap was limited.

We were known as the Smooth Boyz. We thought we could be the next cutting-edge, underground rap sensation. There was me, the Pumpmaster. There was my other white friend, Kevin, aka Bone, aka Vanilla Godzilla. There was our Pakistani friend, known as the Pakistani Powerhouse, or PP. And finally there was our friend Harold, who happened to be black. His rap name was . . . Harold. He knew we were idiots.

We recorded songs in a basement over popular rap instrumentals and competed in battles of the bands. Smooth Boyz won a few competitions, but what we never realized was that most people judging these contests thought we were a *comedy* act and found us hilarious.

Our outfits on stage included bandanas, white tank tops affectionately known as wife-beaters, tear-away nylon pants (we used to rip them off during the chorus of our last song), and headbands—except the headbands weren't on our heads; they were on our necks, like chokers.

Point of clarification: I am not from Queens. I may say this in several rhymes you are about to read, but I have never actually even seen the streets of Queens, though I hear it's very nice.

"This Is It"

Boom, boom, boom—step up in the room.
Pass the microphone and we'll go to the moon,
Cause we fly so high from the rhymes that we write—
And they so tight they make you bounce all night.
Gotta lot to say, name starts with a J,
And hold up, hold on here I go,
I got the crazy, crazy, crazy, freaky, freaky, wild flow.
Stop asking questions cause ya'll boys don't know.
I spit it like a rabbit, fast as shit,
You better stop now, you better quit.
I got the questions to the answers no one knows,
Like who wrote the scriptures and who built the
Alamo.
I spit game so quick like rain so fast—
Ya'll boys can't even say my name.
What?
It's Jakenile, get it right fool because I ain't no tool.

"Smooth Boyz Anthem: Takin' Ova"

Just pass the mic over here for a minute,
I got some crazy words and I'd like to spit it.
I'm the craziest rapper you ever did see,
And I rhyme all these words with the greatest of ease.
Straight up off the mean streets of Queens,
I'm a big time, big huge rapping machine.

My words flow like an Elizabethan sonnet—
And all that money?
My name is on it.
So I'm 6-foot-high,
So alive,
I'll make you cry from the rhymes I derive.
Steppin' to me is like stepping to Bruce Lee—
I'm a master of rap like he was in karate.
Bring the heat on in like a microwave,
Step on in we got the flavor you crave.
Smooth Boyz?
Don't want none of us,
Comin' straight on through like a Greyhound bus.

"What You Gon' Do Now?"

(Song about a drug addict I never even knew)
You messed it up man, look what you did.
You had the nice car, the wife and the kids.
But that's gone now, don't know what to do—
Maybe you would if you weren't such a fool.
You didn't know what you had; you had it all.
Shoulda thought of that before you decided to ball.
Runnin' game never got you nowhere,
And don't even say life isn't fair.
Cause you know you had it, had the life,
Never dealt with hardship pain or strife.
You know ya pops, just gave you money,
But you wasted it all on ice and honey.
There's more important things in the way we live—

Just once did you ever think about your kids?
We gotta come down from our cloud and stop being
so damn proud.
There's gotta be more to livin' than this—
Just try and succeed and live to exist.
To figure out life man, it's real hard.
You gotta have the right deck and play the right cards.
But sometimes—you don't have a full deck,
And sometimes there's nothing to keep you in check.
Sometimes you know the right moves to make—
But others you realize it was a mistake . . .
So what can I say?
Peace, I'm out— it's Jake.

ADULT ME SAYS

Sadly, the Smooth Boyz broke up upon entering college because any time we played a song for a roommate, classmate, or cute girl, they laughed in our faces. This time, we got it.

THE RODEO DRIVE DIET

Lori Gottlieb

I was a scrawny kid and weighed like three pounds when I got my first diary at age eleven. I guess what you should know is that I grew up in the mecca of appearance-obsessed culture. Not just LA—specifically Beverly Hills. But I was far more interested in things like chess and math, and I thought everyone's obsession with appearance was ridiculous.

Julie's mom is always on some new diet, but if you want my opinion, she never looks like she's losing any weight. Her stomach is total BLUBBER. But the rest of her is super skinny, like those pictures of starving kids in Africa with the fat belly but the skinny arms and legs. Except Julie's mom also also has a turkey chin.

Personally, I don't think a diet is gonna help her.

I know all about her diets because Julie BORES me to death talking about them!! All of Julie's mom's diets have these really phony names like "The No Temptation Diet" or "The Effortless Diet" or "Thin in THREE Days." This one's called "The Authentic Movie Star Diet," I guess so people will think that everyone who's a movie star has been following this diet for years. Which is baloney, because most movie stars eat at fancy restaurants all the time. Trust me, I know. I live in Beverly Hills, remember?

Anyway, all do you on THE AUTHENTIC MOVIE STAR

DIET is eat one kind of food each week, but you can eat as much of it as you want. This week, Julie's mom is eating only bananas, but she can eat MILLIONS of them if she wants. Next week, she'll eat only meats, then the week after she'll eat only breads. I don't know what comes the next, but it's a really stupid diet. Besides, I saw the Suzanne Sommers, the actress who plays Chrissy from the show *Three's Company* when I was shopping with Mom at Saks yesterday. She's a movie star, and I really doubt SHE (sarcastic) eats just bananas for a week straight.

Anyway, today Julie said SHE might go on The Authentic Movie Star Diet too. I told Julie that I didn't think she was fat, but Julie said her mom wants her to lose some weight so she won't be chubby and sad as a teenager. Right now Julie's on the "The No Temptation Diet" . . . Which isn't working, because Julie STEALS MUFFINS from the cafeteria now! The first time I saw Julie steal a muffin I almost called this hotline for abused kids because I thought it was sad that Julie's mom was starving her. But Julie's mom can scream pretty loud, which is why I wouldn't want her to know if I reported her. I definitely wouldn't want her to come over to my house and scream at me after school!! I'd DIE. If I didn't die from the noise, I'd probably die from her smelly breath. It smells like . . . . bananas mixed with puke?

Plus, whenever I eat dinner over at Julie's now, her mom says, "Now girls, remember always to leave the table wanting a little something more." Which makes no sense, because the whole POINT of eating is to make you FULL again. DUH!!

And now Mom started doing it too. I was in the kitchen baking cookies after school and when I reached for a second one, Mom told me to save the cookies for "the guys." She was talking about Dad and my brother. I asked Mom why I should save the cookies for David since he never has to save desserts for me. She said that "David's a growing boy and he needs his energy." So I asked Mom why I didn't need to eat the same food since I'm a growing girl. I mean, I'm not gonna be 4'8" for the rest of my life, thank you very much!! But Mom just told me to stop asking "why" all the time. So I didn't ask "why" when I went downstairs before bed and found Mom standing over the kitchen sink stuffing chocolate chip cookies into her mouth.

But the other thing is that whenever we're in a restaurant and Mom can't finish her food, she offers it to David and Dad, but never to me. She just dumps it on their plates while she's telling them how FULL she is. Which OBVIOUSLY can't be true, because if she was so FULL . . . she wouldn't sneak down to the kitchen late at night to stuff cookies into her mouth!

I'm never going on a diet. Not in my entire life. I mean, why would anyone starve themselves on purpose?

ADULT ME SAYS

And then, a few months later, I became anorexic. Go figure. I was admitted to the pediatric ward at Cedars-Sinai Medical Center. Everyone else had tragic diseases like leukemia and cystic fibrosis, and the doctors didn't quite know what to do with the girl who simply wouldn't eat. So my psychiatrist, Dr. Gold, thought he came up with an idea to help me see

how skinny I was. When I wrote the following, I weighed less than sixty pounds.

Today Dr. Gold told me that he's decided to FILM me! I'm serious!! Like, in a movie!! Dr. Gold wants to film me so I can take a good look at myself. I told Dr. Gold that all I do all day is look at myself—that's how I know I'm fat, duh!—but he said seeing myself in a movie would make me look different. (pause) I wonder if it'll make me look skinnier! I hope so!!

Dr. Gold told me they'll probably film me tomorrow, so I can be used as a "case study." That means other doctors will watch it to learn about anorexia. Then Dr. Gold said I'm an "excellent case," which is why they picked me in the first place. I couldn't believe it! I guess that means I'm an excellent dieter. I guess I'm the best dieter at my school, and I'm probably the best dieter in the country . . . maybe even the WORLD!! I mean, I must be, because they want to make a MOVIE of me.

But what if I'm not? I mean, what if the doctors watching my movie have seen thinner anorexics than me? Dr. Gold showed me pictures of anorexics today because he thought it would scare me to know I was as skinny as them, but they were WAY skinnier than I am. I mean, if THAT's what an anorexic looks like, I'm definitely NOT an "excellent case." That's why I'm not eating anything until after the filming tomorrow. Not one bite.

The Next Day
I couldn't sleep last night because I was so EXCITED about starring in my anorexia movie and becoming the most famous

anorexic in the country! I wondered if I'd get to meet my favorite movie stars . . . or even Andy Gibb!! I'd DIE if I met Andy Gibb! Plus, I only had one sip of <u>orange juice</u> since yesterday so I'd look like an excellent case. I didn't want to be a fat anorexic, especially since I found out people look ten pounds fatter in movies.

But when Dr. Gold came today, he didn't have a movie camera or a microphone or anything like I expected. He was only carrying his stupid note pad. He said he decided not to do the movie with me after all. That's because he said I got too excited about it, and it would just make me happy about being too skinny.

I tried to tell him that I'm an excellent case, and I even told him I'm such an excellent case that I didn't even eat anything since yesterday—not one bite!—but Dr. Gold said this was exactly why he wouldn't film me.

What a LIAR!! I'll bet the REAL reason is that I'm too fat after all. But it's my own fault. I mean, I NEVER should have had that sip of orange juice.

ADULT ME SAYS

And then I fired him.

MESSAGE FROM THE MARGINS (PT. 1)

Stacey Grenrock Woods

Like most eleven-year-olds, I thought I was very deep. I thought I had sparkling wit and a keen eye for observation—like a tween Garrison Keillor. Unfortunately, upon revisiting my journals, I realized I was not as wise as I'd imagined.

Stacey on . . . Time
Tuesday is an OK day. Not great though. It's sort of like Monday. Only . . . a day later.

Stacey on . . . The Media
The news. It's okay the first time you watch it . . . but when you watch it two times in a row you want to throw up.

Stacey on . . . Longing
I can't *wait* until I get to 7th grade so I can buy things from the catering truck for lunch!

Stacey on . . . Celebrity
I can do impressions of some people very well. Not always famous people. Just everyday people! Except for Glorida Vanderbilt. Who I do perfectly. You will have to see it sometime.

Stacey on . . . Conformity
I think it's so stupid that a group of girls in the 6th grade will only let you be friends with them if you have a certain label on your pants namely Chemin De Fer.

Stacey on . . . Discrimination
The problems of small and narrow feet. When you have small feet, you can't get high heels like all the other girls, because they think if you have small feet you're younger and all they have are babyish shoes for you!

Stacey on . . . Celebrity Endorsements
Florence Henderson makes me sick with her "Wessonality".

Stacey on . . . Personal Identity
I like to think up stage names. Jaquenline Shell. Robin Peterson. Jennnete Moore. Kami Stapleton. Morgan.

Stacey on . . . Embracing Rock 'N' Roll . . . Almost
I am learning how to play "Stairway to Heaven" . . . on the piano!

Stacey on . . . Harsh Realities
It would be pretty if it really snowed those big exaggerated and delicate snowflakes. But all we see are little white specks.

Stacey on . . . Science
Noise is like the air being filled with sounds . . . that you hear.

Stacey on . . . Daylight Savings

I know we have to have a time change. But it gets so confusing. I don't know why but the year before, everyone had to explain it to me.

Stacey on . . . Leisure Time

I think those girls who do all their homework during recess are pretty stupid. That's the only time in school you are free to talk and play and do other things. I mean, why do you think they call it HOMEwork?

Stacey on . . . The Little Things

Carpeting. Thick and fluffy. Or thin and long. Soft and puffy. Or durable and strong. Carpeting.

Stacey on . . . Never Exceeding Obligations

Well, I've done my 8 pages this week! Bye!

DURAN DURAN FAN FICTION

Jillian Griffiths

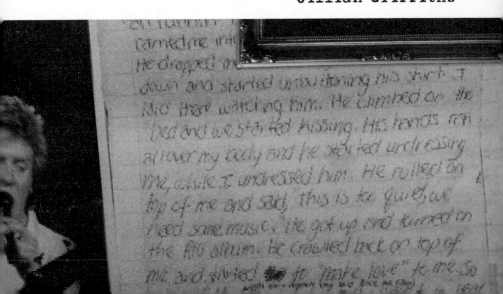

When I was thirteen, I was *obsessed* with Duran Duran, especially John Taylor. My friend Hope and I used to write ten-to-twenty-page fantasies about these "sex gods" and then trade them and read each other's. These outlandish stories were my sweet escape.

When I wrote these imaginings, I believed that these were situations that *actually could* happen—that John Taylor and Simon Le Bon, upon meeting me, could actually fall instantaneously in love with a brace-faced thirteen-year-old girl. As if.

I must remind you that at this time Duran Duran was at the pinnacle of their career, the playboys of their time, and yet, *I believed*. Aside from the dramatic hijinks and escapades, I describe the sex in great detail that could only come from a sexually inexperienced teen.

Some family vacation! My parents and I go away and rent a condo just for one weekend. Some little assholes were playing around with fire crackers and it got out of control. They threw it in our garbage which caught fire and finally lit the whole condo on fire! With my sleeping parents in it! I was out at a bar trying to meet someone nice when I was told my parents had died in a fire from smoke inhalation.

At the hospital, I sat in the waiting room with my face buried in my hands. I heard voices walking by. I looked up and saw John, Roger and Andy Taylor from Duran Duran. John stopped and looked and stared at me. He started following me. What a weird situation! My parents who loved me and raised me have just died. And my future full of happiness was following me. I don't know whether to break down and cry or rejoice. I caught a glimpse of John peeping from behind a corner watching me. I laughed to myself. John came over and sat down. My palms got all sweaty.

"Care to tell me why you're here?" he asked.

"My parents died in a fire while we were vacationing here."

He replied with the usual, "I'm really sorry," but it made me feel A LOT better. "My father had a mild heart attack and that's why I'm here."

"I hope he feels better soon."

John offered me a ride to a hotel and invited me to lunch the next day. I wore my powder blue spring overalls with a blouse. Simon joined us. It was really fun and it took my mind off of my parents. Afterwards we decided to walk along the river. John clasped onto my and hand and we strolled along the path, just the three of us. I felt as if my life was now complete. We went back to their penthouse and went out onto the balcony with a bottle of wine. John said, "I'm worried about you."

"What a guy," I thought.

"How about staying with us? We have plenty of room." Simon was getting excited too.

I said no at first but they made me change my mind.

Nick seemed to like me so he liked the idea of me moving in. And then he said,

"John <u>really</u> likes you. You've known each other just for a day and he hasn't stopped talking about you! I can tell you guys are gonna last. Most of John's girlfriends, the few he's had, were all snots and stuck-up bitches. None of us—me Simon, Roger and Andy—have never liked them, especially Simon. But you're different and you're very nice and pretty. Nothing is gonna stand in John's way from winning you over anybody else who comes along. But I can tell Simon likes you a lot too."

For dinner, me and John made lasagna. Simon, Nick and Roger were trying to make a salad. Simon was peeling a carrot with the wrong side of the peeler, Roger was singing opera with a spaghetti strainer over his head and Andy was hysterical while throwing salad at Roger. Poor Simon was covered with salad and he couldn't figure out how to use the "bloody carrot peeler!" I showed Simon how to use the peeler and he laughed sarcastically. John apologized for their behavior. Nick made pina coladas and then we all watched reruns of *Saturday Night Live*. It was funny. They all got a big kick out of the *Coneheads*.

Then it was time for bed.

"So where am I gonna sleep tonight?" I asked John.

"In bed of course with me. That is if you don't mind?"

"No. Of course I don't mind, but will the others?"

"Nah. They won't care at all."

John was lying on the bed smiling at me in a very sexy and eager way. He poured a glass of wine and we both drank from it at the same time. Kinky, huh? We looked deep into each other's eyes and alas, our lips came closer. Our tongues met in a fascinating sensation. Our tongues danced, jumped and twisted around in our mouths which were "all runnin' inside." Our kiss was slow and beautiful, not like you see in dirty movies when everything is fast and complicated, not to mention gross. He turned the lights down and started unbuttoning his shirt.

"This is too quiet. We need some music." He got up and turned on the *RIO* album. He climbed on top of me like a baby tiger. Gentle but sort of aggressive. By now everything was off except for his bandana and we started to make love. So what if the flow of his body wasn't in beat with the music. He created a wonderful performance which lasted one whole side of *RIO* plus the other side up to *Save a Prayer*. Everything went slowly even when we reached the farthest point of intercourse. He pushed harder but it felt so good. Finally our love-making came to a stop and John rolled off of me.

In the kitchen the next morning, Simon greeted me full of pep. I was surprised he didn't have a hangover.

"Nooo. I'm used to it," he said. "So, you really like John, huh? I mean . . . oh, never mind," he said with a sigh.

"No. What were you going to say?" I questioned him.

"I just wanted to know if you liked me like you like John, cause . . . I really like you . . . a lot. John is gonna have a hard time winning you over." I couldn't believe my ears! "Simon. Listen. I love John even though we just met. And I love you as a great friend."

His eyes looked sad but I knew he wouldn't give up. "Can't you forget John just for one night?"

"No. I can't." I felt terrible.

A little later, John answered the phone and turned pale.

Gayle, his older sister had been in a car accident and was in a coma. John, Roger and Andy flew home to see her. Then, just my luck, Nick had to leave because he was producing an album for Kajagoogoo.

Me and Simon were left alone.

Simon said, "How about going to the beach?"

"Sure," I replied.

He knew a private beach so we were just about the only people on it. This was the first time I really got a look at Simon's body. There was no freckle OR scar on that tan, muscular, body. I asked Simon to put some suntan lotion on my back. He started massaging my back so gently and then he picked me up and ran right into the cold water with me! Finally, he just held me and looked longingly at my lips. I could see his eager tongue moving around inside his mouth and then I felt it inside of my mouth! He used his tongue almost as good as John.

"Let's get outta here," he said.

We went straight home and went straight to bed. I couldn't believe what I was doing. He undressed me and himself. He too had turned on music but his beat was much more in time and stronger than John's. He sure weighed more than John. We had some really mean sex and after it was all over, me and Simon talked.

"Please don't tell John we ever did this. I love him too much and I just don't want him or anybody else to know."

Simon understood and promised not to tell <u>and</u> that it won't happen again. Even though we both <u>loved</u> it.

I missed John so much, I missed his security, his strength, his love.

We were all out at dinner one night and as were walking to the car, a total JACKASS! came zooming by and hit DEAR JOHN! He was unconscious. Roger ran to call an ambulance.

At the hospital, the doctor came out and said, "We've done everything we could. I'm sorry."

I went hysterical. I ran to Simon's open arms. All of the guys' eyes were flooded with tears.

"You know he loved you," Nick said soothingly.

We went in to see him. I looked at John lying there, so helpless with tubes coming out of his arms. "What's the use?" I screamed to myself. His face was so innocent and so was he. "God, if you can hear me, please listen. This wonderful, religious person has done nothing to deserve this pain. Neither have I. I love him and he loves me. Create some miracle so this person, this human being may live!"

Simon had tears rolling down his face. It was over. I no longer had anything to live for in my life. But then, I felt a twitch in John's hand. He was trying to SQUEEZE MY HAND!!

"I love you, I love you." HE SPOKE!

"He's gonna make it!" shouted the doctor. There must have been a small miracle." John whispered, "Before I fall asleep, I wanted to know if you want to marry me?" It came out slow but I understood it.

"Yes! I would love to!"

John said, "Good because I really love you." And then he fell asleep.

ADULT ME SAYS

It's ironic that now if there is one celebrity I see more than any other running around Los Angeles, it's John Taylor. Hello, John!

THE MISSIONARY
IMPOSITION

Kirsten Gronfield

When I was in junior high school, I had a best friend named Chelsea, and I wanted to be just like her. She was the coolest, in every way . . . except one. I was worried that Chelsea wasn't a Christian.

I was determined to save her soul, but I wasn't sure exactly *how* to do it. So I sought out an answer from a girl I barely knew but had met at a Christian camp.

Dear Christi,

Hey! I'm not quite sure whether or not you remember me, probl'y not. Well, to refresh your memory, my name's Kirsten Gronfield. You may have my address from Music Minnesota, which is how we met, if that wasn't obvious! Oh well, on a slightly more detailed note, I'm about 5'6", blond, blue-eyed, had a cousin from Nebraska, stepsister (Marta) and, let's see, I sat by you during the pizza party. Well, even if you hadn't met me, you probably would have some kind of idea of who I was/ am (which is right *was* or *am*?) now.

Anyway, how're you? Well, I am, hmmm, a little kooky at this moment. I'm at our 115 year old home's dining room listening to Christian musician Al Denson.

(If ever there was someone who added meaningless information to a messy, odd letter, it was I . . . is I . . . whatever)

As you can probably tell English (technical that is) isn't my strong suit. I actually love to write (only humorously, I'm not that serious . . . mosta the time!)

So how's Texas doin'?

Not to change the subject (which is exactly what I'm about to do) BUT . . . somewhere along the line I was going to mention my own surprise and awe in the fact that I am actually writing a letter to someone (not including the notes I scribble to my friends during class!

Boy, I just go on and on! This Sunday I'm singin' "O Sifuni Mungu" in church w/ the trax! (Not alone of course) (then again I have done that while vacuuming more than once!) (Do you by any chance know how to spell "vacuum"?)

"Tested by Fire" is on the radio. I love this song, of course I love all of them. This one really hits me.

This "predicament" is partly why I'm writing, unfortunately not just to chat!

See here, my best friend, Chelsea, believes in God, I think, but she doesn't go to church, doesn't believe "a lot of what's in the Bible," and won't listen to any Christian music because it's Christian, and won't be in our church musical even though she loves acting.

Anyway. I was kind of hoping you may have a solution for me. I've found some music that's just exactly like her "unchristian" (I guess you could call it) music, but I don't have enough money to buy it if she won't look at it if she even suspects it's Christian. What should I do? Any ideas (other than shooting her) (which is tempting) (j/k) would be wonderful.

Anyway, to undampen my light-hearted letter, I must tell

you I have a sore finger or two from squeezing the pencil for so long! Please write, even if not about Chelsea, it would be terrific to hear from ya!

Bye now,

Almost a stranger,

Kirsten

(referred to as soybean, Little one, and baby ghost by my sister)

outside of that "dork" applies for most.

Well only my friends as a joke only of course.

Well, I'll let your eyes have a rest (actually stopping is completely under a selfish motive considering my arm/hand pain.)

R.S.V.P. did you know that R.S.V.P. stands for

Respondez Sil vous Plait

(French)

Respond, Please

(English)

We don't waste a breath in the good old US of A!

Kirsten

I guess I already wrote my name.

ADULT ME SAYS

Well, I *never* heard back from Christi, but I still needed to save Chelsea! She was my best friend (other than Jesus). So there was only one thing I could do.

I would write a song for Chelsea myself. And in composing

it, I would keep in mind her favorite groups: the Cure and Jane's Addiction.

Chorus
> Look at all the Lord has blessed us with
> And we turn around and abuse his gift.
> Look how the Lord tells us how he cares
> And we turn away with silent stares.

Verse 1
> When God made Adam he gave him a pleasurable mouth,
> But now we use it to shout
> And constantly we block him out.
> God did not give voice to Adam for use of sin
> We have speech and song for praising him

(Chorus)

Verse 2
> When God made us able to feel
> It was to touch someone, and love, and heal
> But every day our hands are used as punishment
> To demonstrate anger and build up walls of resent
> To slap, to hit, to punch to steal
> Have we <u>ever</u> used our hands to feel?

(Chorus)

136

Verse 3

Smelling is a gift that proves
That humans can abuse whatever they chose
To plug your nose and say "you stink"
C'mon everybody let's all sit and think
The Lord didn't give us sense of smell
To comfort us in the darkness of hell
But as a pleasure, what did we use it for?
To hurt, to tease, and make others' souls sore.

(Chorus 2X "Everybody!")

ADULT ME SAYS

I showed her the song and she finally converted . . . to a
new best friend.

LETTER TO MY FUTURE SELF

Kirsten Gronfield

When I was in eighth grade, my teacher gave me an assignment to write a letter to my "future self." At the time, I had no idea just *who* she'd grow up to be. A teacher? An heiress? A failure? A success? I only knew her name and the name of her pet pony (Purple Island).

Dear Self,

Are you still me? It may seem like an odd question, but I am really hoping that the answer is clear.

Are you still the one who refuses to brush her teeth after drinking orange juice in the morning? Do you still have a scar from flipping off your bike? Are you still dreaming of stage lights?

Do you often enjoy frolicking *purely* on whims?

Do you still taste ideas? Twirl them around on your tongue? Are trees still the most *marvelous* things you see?

Do you remember the first time you came to school here? Can you still feel *the hurt*?

Do you still think it's a toss up between Sean Connery, Harrison Ford, and Christian Slater for sexiest man alive? Do you still feel incredibly shallow for mentioning that?

Are you still me?

Do you still believe you have the ability to "*do it all*"? Are

you still trying to fulfill the unquenchable urge to learn how to
. . . throw a pot?

Can you really have finished high school? Are you scared of
being a shadow? Is your heart not easily broken?

Are you still me?

Do you remember the time you went to see "Les Miserables"?
When you see it now, do you remember to *breathe*?

When no one is home, do you sing your heart out till it
hurts? Have you still the secret desire to dream alone?

When was the last time you defined yourself on a dreary
day as a pebble furrowed in dark, hard clay?

Are you still a Christian? Have you saved anyone? Did
you ever feel the strength to show someone "the way" like I'm
hoping? How could we *ever* disbelieve?

Do you still laugh as you read your horoscope? Do you still
feel the hunger to enjoy everyone? Are you gasping for life?

Are you still me?

Can you even picture me? Your evil twin? Or are you *my*
evil twin? My twin at all?

Are you confident? Do you ever have reason to fear? Have
you met the man of your dreams? Who *are* your friends?
Where's Carolyn? Did you get a scholarship? Have you hugged
mom recently? Dad? Have you developed *any* talent?

Are you who you want to be?

Just how much have we changed, myself? Are you quite
sure you've grown up at all? Are you still me?

O I FUCKIN CANT
IS BASTARD CAMP I
what I SAID when
here AND you r-ther
sten To th
To SCrEAM o
...ready. Scr
..dy in this
ert. I DOn

(Eariipcham)
like me HOme
you cont get me out
wehr, im gonna HATE your guts &
Forgive A For weeks.
on my FIRST overnight Hike,
-one night it rained

UNHAPPY CAMPER

Adam Gropman

Growing up in a suburb close to Boston, I was a real city kid—a homebody. I mean, I left the house to ride my bike around or hang out with my friends, but I preferred to stay within like a one-mile radius if I could help it. There was nowhere else I wanted to be.

When I turned ten, my parents decided to toughen me up. They sent me to a rustic summer camp in Vermont for two months. The place had no electricity, no running water. The cabins had only three walls. And campers were strongly encouraged to swim naked, as the native Indians had. It was like a POW camp for kids whose only crime was growing up in the liberal suburbs.

The following is some correspondence from that summer between myself and my parents.

July 1, 1976 (First Day)

Dear Mom & Dad,

I am fine. Today I tried the swimming test. I only made it across the docks two times. Dinner is <u>great</u> here!

P.S. I made a lot of friends and one especially named Peter.

July 5, 1976

Dear Mom and Dad camp is good!

And the food is great! Also, when I said I only did two laps between docks, I did four . . . and I practiced to do <u>six</u>!

P.S. I'm kind of homesick so please visit as soon as you can.

July 10, 1976

Dear Adam:

Boy did we love your letter!! We read it to <u>everybody</u>!! I am proud of your swimming improvement. It sounds like you must be a dock swimmer by now. We are having a feud with the squirrels because they are eating the peaches.

Love and kisses, Mom.

ADULT ME SAYS

My dad then added a little drawing and wrote, "Have you seen Irving the Duck?"

July 11, 1976

Mom + Dad,

I have a very bad cold and I feel very sick. <u>This</u> is what's wrong. I have a bad sore throat. My nose and sinus are very stuffy. I have awful headaches. I feel <u>very</u> weak. Everybody, except for two people in this cabin, are assholes. Right at this moment, while I'm writing this letter, someone's teasing me and saying I'm faking to be sick.

I also lost my knife and my flashlight <u>still</u> doesn't work.

Later That Night

Dear Mom + Dad,

I can't hack camp any longer. I'm going to have a screaming mental fit. By the way, what I mean by "take me out of this camp" is come up here in the car and take me HOME! I hate this goddamn cabin. I want to see our house and sleep in <u>my</u> nice, comfortable bed and sleep till 10:30 instead of waking up at 7:00!

July 13, 1976

Dear Adam:

I guess you have gone through some sad and difficult days. I think it would be better for you NOT to worry about your clothes and flashlight and things. As Alfred E Neuman says: "Why worry?"

Maybe when you are really angry at the world, you could go to some private place in the woods . . . and cry about it (that's good) or <u>yell at the trees</u> (they won't mind). And when you come back from hollering and hitting the ground with a stick, you won't feel angry.

Love, Mom

July 16, 1976

Dear Mom and Dad,

Camp is shitty and boring. Everything's been going wrong. Such as:

Jason borrowed my red short-sleeved shirt and lost it.

My flashlight (still) isn't working.

I got a cut on my penis when I flunked my canoe test.

I'm <u>very</u> homesick. I wish you could arrange so I can only stay 1 month instead of 2.

What I left out from that list was that Eddie, the kid in the bunk bed over me, had accidentally dropped toothpaste down on me and then dropped a candle, which lit my blanket on fire.

July 14, 1976

Dear Adam,

I'm sorry that you hurt your penis. Does it still bother you?

Love-Dad

July 19, 1976

Dear Mom + Dad,

I fuckin' can't stand this bastard camp! You better goddamn listen to this letter or I'm going to scream! And as a matter of fact, I already screamed my ass off at everybody in this cabin today. I don't goddamn understand why you don't believe that I'm having a conniption! Now I know you hate my guts, because if you liked me, you wouldn't torture me. Come up here on Saturday the 24th. If you send me one more of those crap letters, I'll rip it up and burn it.

July 21, 1976

Dear Adam:

Did you get the comics? Things around here are pretty boring.

Love, Mom

July 26, 1976

Dear Mom and Dad,

I can't stand it anymore!!! All the kids in my cabin hate me! They steal and wreck up my things! I can't escape it! I want . . . to go . . . KILL MYSELF!!!!

July 28, 1976

Dear Adam,

Yesterday Garth, Willie and Peter said "glub glub" when I added water to their tank. Chi Chi and Bianco are fine. The red efts are doing well. That's all for now.

Love,
Daddy

July 29, 1976

Dear Mom,

I'm . . . going . . . CRAZY. Camp is shitty and everybody in the whole camp <u>hates</u> me! How can I take 29 more days?

Aug 1, 1976

Dear Adam,

Think about something . . . you feel really good about.

And then before you know it, you won't feel like a Gloomy Gus anymore!

Mom

Less than a week after my parents finally came and pulled me out nearly a month early, we received a letter from the camp owners. It was dated the day after I left the camp. The letter informed all parents that due to an accident wherein a camper was playing with matches, a fire quickly spread and burned two cabins to the ground. One of those cabins was mine. And that kid? It was Eddie, my bunkmate from before. The letter went on to explain that campers were now sleeping in the dining room and that any and all donations would be gladly accepted during this unfortunate and challenging time.

So you tell me: sheltered, elementary school cry-baby pussy, or sensitive ten-year-old prophet?

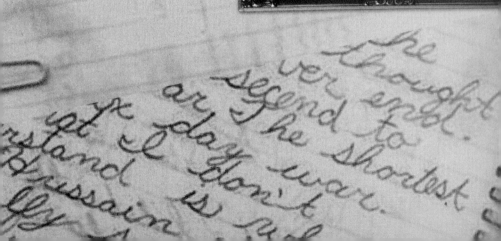

MESSAGE FROM THE MARGINS (PT. 2)

Abby Gross

Until third grade, school was some sort of utopia for me—we played games, learned about penmanship, and had long periods of time during the school day to read silently.

But it was in third grade that I started to pay attention to life within and outside of my classroom, and, like a good American, make sweeping judgments about the world around me. With only bits and pieces of information learned in school and from television, I started to develop alarmingly specious opinions about society, politics, culture, and education. All the while there was the new realization that everyone else seemed to be having a *great* time, while I was sitting quietly and writing in my journal.

What follows are selected sentences from my journal spanning the latter half of third grade.

Abby on . . . Setting Goals

My New Year's resolution is to be more popular in third grade.

Abby on . . . Civil Rights

I wish Dr. Martin Luther King was here at this time. I wish he was president. If Dr. King was here at this time, I wouldn't be afraid of thunder. (Gosh! Am I a scardie cat!!)

Abby on . . . Politics

I think George Washington is very good.

Abby on . . . Education

SCIENCE. I don't think I learn much in science. Once I finish with a paper I forget what I've learned. But I did like learning about drugs. Science is boring.

Abby on . . . World Peace

THE WAR IS OVER! I am glad the war is over. I thought it would never end. This is the second to shortest war. What I don't understand is why Saddam Hussein gave up. He really surprised me! I wonder what place he'll invade next?

Abby on . . . Observing Peer Groups

I would fit in more with a school of fish.

Abby on . . . Dispelling Myths

I think Santa Claus is really Sam Cooperman, and he dresses up and brings presents to orphans and children in hospitals. When I grow up, I want to sell chocolate-covered pretzels. I think my business will be good. Why? Because a lot of people like chocolate-covered pretzels.

Abby on . . . Animal Rights . . . and Wrongs . . .

I really really wish my stuffed animals would come alive. I really really wish my cat would talk to me and not turn away when I try to teach her how to talk. My cat scratched Amy yesterday when Amy put smelly cream in her face. Then Amy put smelly cream in my face and chased me down the stairs.

Abby on . . . Feminism
I felt different when these girls came to play outside and they all knew each other and I didn't know them. They were all good friends. Women!

Abby on . . . Diversity
Indians. I would like the cooking part of being Indian, but not the rest. Don't they ever get tired? All those languages and confusions. I bet it would be hard!

Abby on . . . The Upside of Violent Societies
I think the medieval times were very good. They had: singers, minstrels, magicians, jugglers, jesters, puppeteers, acrobats, dancers, queens, kings, princesses, and princes. Not to mention mummies.

Abby on . . . Futility
I HATE SOCIAL STUDIES! I will like life now better that I don't have to do boring workbook pages. If you don't want the book I will throw it away. Then it will haunt me. Well I don't care as long as it's gone. Social studies is the worst part of the day. It's dumb to learn the same stuff year after year. Next year we learn about climates. What do you think is more boring, communities, families, or climates? What's the point of school if you just learn the same thing? It's torture, and then we still don't know anything.

IN LIKE

Mathew Harawitz

When I was fourteen, I kept a diary. I wish it had been a *journal*, but it was a *diary*. In fact, the only thing remotely masculine about it is my sloppy handwriting.

I was a social kid, but not remotely popular. My group of friends were very important to me. We were all "girl crazy." Unfortunately, girls weren't "us crazy." But of all my friends, I was the girl craziest, and I had to find a girl who would no longer let my crazy go unrequited.

I loved being "in *like*"—not love, *like*. Like is pretty much love with training wheels. I liked sitting around with my friends figuring out how we were going to get the girl we *liked* to *like* us. After those plans didn't work out, I liked finding a new girl to *like*. And, most of all, I liked writing about all of it . . . in my diary.

By the way, here's a quick clarification: A conclave, as used here, is a Jewish youth group sleepover, where temples from all over New York would ship their kids to another temple to spend the weekend.

10-14

Well, the conclave is over and it made baseball history. I met so many people including Flo. On the bus home from the hayride we made out and I got to third. I didn't know if we were "going out" or not, but she cleared that up on the bus. "I'm just out of a bad relationship," she said, but I got what I wanted . . .NOT. Well, no pain no gain. Its fun while it lasted. I met Jessica, Meredith, and Karen. 2 of which I'll call. Remember: On conclave just because you make out doesn't mean you're going out.

10-15

Today, everything changed! No more Flo, Regan or even Rena. Today I discovered Randi (Welch that is). I don't know why . . . she was just over there, but today she was here. I have to tell someone. A big change will happen tomorrow. I'm moving to a new lunch table. From Gregg, Tyler and Scott to Andy's table. I don't know why? I'll give Randi a chance and talk to Sharon about it. Speaking of Sharon, I never thought of her that way. I don't know why? I tell her everything and her, me. They say you marry your best friend. It could be a sign. Well, I am but a star in the Universe, sometimes I feel like a galaxy.

10-16

4 pm . . . Early Edition

I was watching MTV and saw a video called "Can't Stop Fallin' In Love" by Cheap Trick. It made me wonder . . . over the last month I've liked many a girl. So what's wrong? I'm not horny or desperate. To recap, it's been Lisa, Rena, Regan, and now it's Randi. And how can I forget Fast Flo. I gotta talk to Sharon about this maybe get some inside info. No saying at this time.

5:30 . . .

Today I was talking to Scott and I got the real Flo story. Everything she said was true except she didn't like the fact she

met me 20 minutes before. I like quickies . . . the fact is I tried
to believe I didn't love her . . . fact is I did.

10-17

In Social Studies today I began to think of a question he asked
us to think about. It was who are the 5 most influential people
in our lives. I put:

1. Scott
2. Adam
3. Andy
4. Sharon
5. Gregg or Mel

ADULT ME SAYS

Mel was my therapist.

6. Amy

When I gave it more thought, 1 and 2 were tied, 3 and 4
also. 5a at one time was one. But as I think about it it's . . . 1.
Adam 2. Scott 3. Amy 4. Andy and the rest just aren't clear. It
seems friends come and go, but I can't keep up. Adam and I
were unseperable at one time. Then, for some dumb reason I got
sick of him, now we're back I think. Then "Doogie Howser, MD"
came on and I thought everyone seems to be a sidekick. Which
made me think am I sidekick or do I have a sidekick? Am I the
Doogie and am I the Vinnie? Between Andy and Scott I am one,
but I still think for myself. But as Gregg and Ian are concerned

I have a sidekick. But now my thought deepened I thought is it really fair to have stages of friends. Everyone has it (a Best Friend I mean). You think each year you have a different one or you have seen too much of one and they get annoying (sometimes). School seems to cause this, if you're not in someone's class you don't get to see them and thus the friendship can't strengthen. And Vice Versa. No saying tonight, I'm too confused!!!!

10-20

Irony sucks the yanger! On Thursday 3rd period before I was gonna ask out Regan, Lisa told me she broke up with her boyfriend. So I didn't ask her out. Then Friday I was so psyched! Sharon was gonna talk to Randi for me. I was gonna hit on Lisa. I had my cool shirt on and everything BUT Sharon was sick. Lisa got back together with her boyfriend. I wore too much cologne. But I got a lot of shirt compliments. Question: Why are so many songs about love?

11-8

What does Reagan have in common with Mr. Ed? They both say "Nay." Yup, she rejected me . . . but with legitimacy.

But they say with every dark night comes a bright day. Well who cares now. I have to wallow in my virginity. The last couple of entries have been short . . . I'm sorry. The book is coming along great.

ADULT ME SAYS

I was writing a novel about Batman.

12-4

Top 3 Wish List

   3. Grow

   2. Lose Weight

   1. She says yes.

ADULT ME SAYS

Still the same three things that run my life.

1-27

Back from winter conclave. Everything went great although everything went opposite of what I thought. Flo was as if she wasn't there. I stayed with Jason Shoenberg. When we got to the temple a shy girl caught my eye. She was so delicate, so beautiful—I fell in love. Well, one thing led to another and I followed her to the first study. Then they moved us to another group. So I made the best of it and later asked her her name. Sharon Unis. I hung out with her and when dance time came along I made my move. I asked if she'd dance and we did. I liked her and vice versa. She stole my heart and I don't ever want it back.

3-15

The day has finally arrived . . . "Pump Up The Volume" is out on Video.

7-17

Ok, I haven't written in a while so here's an update. I passed! Camp has started. It's in week 3 and already 2 loves. First Sandi . . . asked her to the movies and got the nay. Then in teen group I met Janni. Her sister is Maggie (the hottest girl in the history of camp Rosmarins.) Before we even met, I was in Summer love with Janni. She's cute, innocent, lovely and incredible. But now that I know how beautiful, well-built and incredible Maggie is I find myself thinking Janni is the future. She'll be everything Maggie is and more! But I'm only friends with Maggie, nothing more. Janni is also pretty young . . . 14 and she could be a CIT, but she's still a camper. I worry what they will say. I have 6 weeks left. I really want a summer fling. But please Lord I beg for you to help . . . make Janni like me. Please!!!

7-17, Later

I mean I wanna grab her by the arm and say, "Janni I love you. I need you to go out with me." Kiss her and go out til the end of the summer. At first I just wanted a summer fling to fuck at the end of the summer. But now I want a summer relationship. Please Lord grant my wish . . . I want this one to work. PLEASE!

7-26

I swallowed my balls! I went up to her and said look I like you! Would you go out with me?! She wants to think about it. That's as good as No.

So I'm very depressed. The thing is, testosterone is an incomplete hormone, it needs estrogen to be strong.

THE GRASS IS ALWAYS
SETH GREENER

Brianna Jacobson

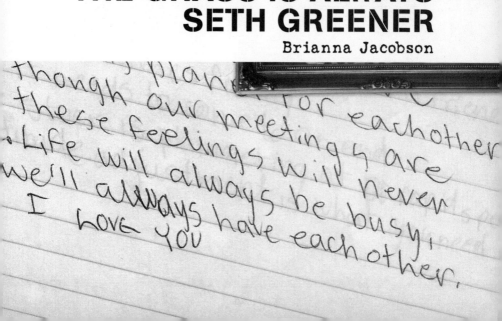

ME & JOSS

I fell in love with actor Seth Green when I was eight years old. Long before *Buffy the Vampire Slayer*, he was on a show called *The Byrds of Paradise*, also starring Timothy Busfield and Jennifer Love Hewitt. Much to my dismay, the show was canceled after a couple of episodes.

Clearly, my love for him should have overpowered the iron fist of any TV exec.

5/29/99

I am in love in an illegal way with Seth Green. Sure he is ten years older than me, but that doesn't matter. He is witty, hot, intelligent, witty, hot, witty, and hot. Did I mention that he is witty and hot? He brightens my day.

Everyone at school knows I am obsessed with him. I bet if we met, we would get along. I want to be a cast member of *Buffy*. That show is the epitome of high school drama. I like Seth more than I like Oz, so I guess I am a good fan.

2/8/01

Happy birthday Seth my love! Wow! You're 26 now you old fart. Still got ten and a half years on me. That doesn't matter though. Never did, never will. We are in love, and that's all that matters. No matter what anyone else says, we are special.

Two of a kind! We were put on this planet for each other. Even though our meetings are brief, these feelings will never change. Life will always be busy, and we'll always have each other. I love you!

2/21/01

I hate you Joss [Whedon] because you always hurt people when things are good. Just when life is a bowl of cherries, it turns sour. Angel turned, Riley and Oz left, and now Joyce is dead! How will Buffy and Dawn support themselves? Buffy has no time to breathe, let alone get a job. Where will they live?

There's no room with Xander in the basement of hell, who wants to live with Giles, and there is no mansion at the end of the yellow brick road. Will Buffy quit school? She doesn't have a driver's license. Who will take care of Dawn? She'll be crushed. I bet Glory did it. The psycho hell bitch warned Buffy. She's just keeping her word.

I want Spike and Buffy to get together. I mean have you seen James? Who would reject that? He's bloody hot! If he was in love with me, I'd have an almost tough time being faithful to Seth. Speaking of Seth, I want Oz back. I only get to see Seth so often, and if he was on *Buffy* again, that's a guaranteed Tuesday night visit with my husband.

Hell, I should just be on *Buffy*, and everything would be okay in the world.

4/10/01

I miss you Seth. Why do you always go away? Hollywood can wait for like five minutes, right? Come back to me my love before my insides melt.

"Seth"

Beauty overwhelms me
Looking at his face
He is far too heavenly
To live in this place
My heart races
Head pounds
I know how corny this all sounds
But he is so special
In every way
I think about him every second
Of every day
His red hair and green eyes
Top off the leather pants
Covering his thighs
I don't know if I could handle
You being my friend
Because I would love you
To the very end
Looking at you is enough
To give me that necessary rush

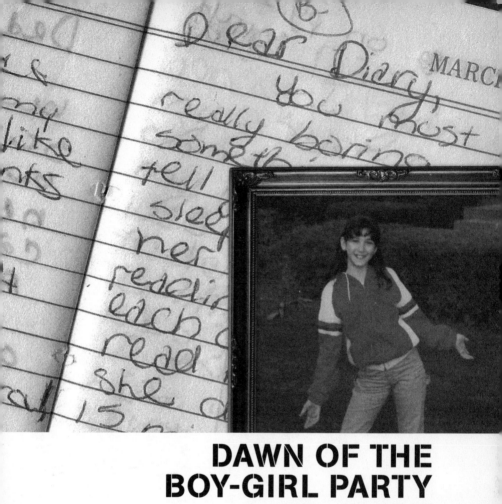

DAWN OF THE
BOY-GIRL PARTY

Sharone Jelden

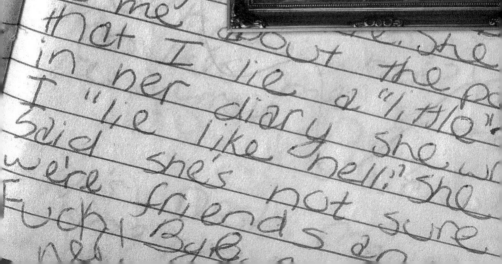

Sixth grade was a year of firsts for me—first kiss, first boy-girl party, first internal parasite. Also, I had to learn how to cope with a bully who used the song "My Sharona" as his intimidation technique. It was a year of rapid maturation, in which my main focus was simply finding a nice boyfriend and coining new usages for the word "bitch."

Dear Diary,

Sorry I had to start so late but I just got you. I just came back from the center with Amy, Beth, and Laura. Laura was a bitch. I got some nice stickers.

I wish I would get invited to a boy-girl party. Ryan Silverman had one, but I wasn't invited because he really hates me.

We have so many tests tomorrow. I think Dan Rosen likes me.

By now,
Sharone
B+ (grade the day)

Dear Diary,

You must think I'm really boring. Well, I have something interesting to tell you. Beth came to sleep over. She brought her diary and we were reading our diaries to each other. I thought she read me everything but she didn't. Well, she went home and about fifteen minutes ago I got the urge to look at it because she left it here on my bed. She read to me about the part that I lie a "little" (which I don't) but in her diary she wrote I "lie like hell." She also said she's not sure if we're friends anymore. Fuck her!

Bye now,
Sharone
B-

Dear Diary,

So much happened today! Michael asked Amy out. (Not anywhere, just to be friends.) And Dan likes me a lot and everyone says he is going to ask me. He even wrote D.R. + S.K. on his desk. Beth is jealous like hell because me and Amy have boyfriends and she doesn't.

Oh yeah—we played our April Fools joke on Miss Waldstein in Social Studies where we all stared at her ankles in class to make her cry. We found out that she's embarrassed of them because they are so skinny. Supposedly if you stare at them long enough she'll step into the waste basket to hide them. That didn't happen though but she did look sad. Then I felt bad for her. Beth said I always feel bad for everyone and that's dumb. Beth is mean like hell.

Bye,
Sharone
A-

Dear Diary,

The Shrinky Dink pins we made in art came out. I made

one rainbow and one that says "Go Red Sox" with a picture of a sock and bat. Ryan said, "Sharone, let me wear your pin with your name on it." Everyone was going, ooooh, Ryan likes Sharone. Then he told everyone that he doesn't like me or my pins.

Amy called Dan for me yesterday. I talked to him for 45 minutes. He said after we go to the center Michael wanted us all to go to Deffazzio Field. You know what I mean.

I asked Dan if he likes Amy and he said he wouldn't go out with her if I paid him! He said he doesn't think she's pretty!

Bye,

Sharone

B+

Dear Diary,

After I had my snack and watched *General Hospital* I made doodie. I wiped myself and these little white worms were on the toilet paper. They were crawling around in the toilet too. I don't think this is very good. I looked it up in Dad's medical book and it said it was pinworm. I think I might have to go to the doctor.

Dan hasn't called or asked me out. I'm getting discouraged.

Bye,

Sharone

C-

Dear Diary,

Guess what! I have exciting news! Dan invited me to Ethan's boy-girl party! It was cancelled though. Dan finally called me!

Twice! We talked for about 10 minutes in all.

Michael invited Amy to Ethan's party. (Before it got cancelled.) She was so excited for a couple minutes. Then I told her it got cancelled.

On the phone Dan asked me if you get presents on Passover! I didn't want to say no but I didn't want to lie so I just laughed. He asked me what's so funny. I hope I didn't offend him.

Bye,

Sharone

A-

Dear Diary,

Dan asked Amy what she thinks he should get me and guess what she said! Underwear! I'll kill her! Then he called me three times and asked me out!

Ryan sang MY SHARONA for the whole recess today. It's been almost two years! I wish that song would go away and Ryan would too.

By the way, I didn't go to the doctor for those living worms.

Love,

Sharone

B+

Dear Diary,

Me, Dan, Amy and Michael all went out! Mom said I could go. Now I'm working on them about letting me go to Ethan's boy-girl party. It's not cancelled anymore.

We went bowling and to McDonalds. Me and Amy were

trying to be mature, but Dan and Michael got Happy Meals. We still had fun though.

After my date I went home and had a pillow fight with my sister and her friend in our basement. I got these shooting pains in my heart and Mom thought I must be having a big heart attack. She rushed me to the hospital and they stuck stuff all over me to check my heart. The way everyone was running around I thought I might die. Then everyone stopped running and they took off all the sticky things.

It turns out I had bad heartburn from the Big Mac and fries and shake I had on my date, plus I might have pulled a muscle during the pillow fight.

Love,

Sharone

A-

Dear Diary,

I'm going to BEG mom to let me go to Ethan's boy-girl party.

Beth got her braces put on today and it makes her lips puff out even more!

I went over to Beth's house for dinner and we did something not so good. We snuck into her parents bedroom while her mom was making dinner and she showed me her dad's newest *Penthouse* magazine. He hides them under the mattress. She showed me it a few times before, but this time her dad caught us when he got home from work. He told her mom. They made us sit down and tell them why we were looking at it. Beth said the pictures were funny and I said I don't know why. I hope they don't tell my mom and dad! My parents will kill me.

Love,
Sharone
B-

Dear Diary,

I don't think mom and dad are going to let me go to the party. They're kind of mad at me and I'm waiting for a punishment right now. I can hear them downstairs fighting about what to do to me. I tried to suggest the hot pepper but they said to go to my room. Beth's mom did tell my mom about the magazine, even though it wasn't my idea. She's awful like hell!

I'm nice enough not to tell them all about how Beth wanted to look at my boobs through some cups, or how I walked in on her parents having sexual intercourse standing up backwards with feathers.

Bye,
Sharone
C

Dear Diary,

MOM AND DAD ARE LETTING ME GO TO THE PARTY! I'm so glad!

And I didn't even get punished!

Love,
Sharone
A

Dear Diary,

Today we had the party! It was okay. No one showed up though.

Just me, Amy, Robin, Dan, Bobby, Ryan and Ethan. Ethan was really depressed because about twenty kids didn't show up. He kept throwing an empty plastic Coke bottle against the wall in his basement. All we did was watch the basketball game and play a couple of kissing games. Ethan has WAY too much spit in his mouth.

I had to spend two minutes in the closet kissing Dan. After I came out I sang that song "I Made It Through The Rain" as a joke. Me and Amy were the only ones who thought it was funny. We couldn't stop laughing until Ethan threw the Coke bottle at us and told us to shut up.

Love,

Sharone

A-

Dear Diary,

Me and Dan broke up I think. He's in a really bad mood about it. He wouldn't stop playing butt ball so the teacher had to come get him. It's okay, he didn't have a good sense of humor. Not to be mean, but he wasn't the greatest looking thing either.

I hope I find someone else.

Ryan was such a jerk at recess. He wouldn't pick me, Beth or Laura to play basketball and when I finally got to play he told everyone not to pass the ball to me. I wanted to kick him where it counts!

(I didn't).

Love,

Sharone

C+

P.S. The Celtics won the playoffs today!

Dear Diary,

I'm really sorry I haven't been keeping up with you. The Celtics won the championship!

As for boys, I am going out with Derek now. We went to the carnival yesterday. We only went on one ride together but he held my hand. Tonight was the talent show. I wasn't in it but I was an usher. The cast party was really fun. We had a food fight.

Ryan started singing, "Da na na na na na na na" so I threw a bowl of fruit salad at him. Hurray for me!

Love,

Sharone

B+

CHEAP JEW

Sharone Jelden

While I was growing up, my family's financial situation resembled *The Jeffersons*, except we were white, Jewish, and lacking that great theme song. Even without the song, my parents built a thriving business from nothing. By the time I reached high school, I was labeled one of the "rich kids." This made me feel "wicked self-conscious." I longed to trade in our swimming pool and Volvo for a patch of concrete and an old station wagon.

My absurd phobia at age seventeen was that being rich and Jewish could lead to being labeled "a cheap Jew" if I didn't hand out cash or buy hot lunches for my classmates. So instead of enjoying my parents' success and generosity, I spent most of high school afraid the other kids would ostracize me. Hate me. Egg my house *again*.

I would have relished the opportunity to be poor and Catholic. . . . I thought it would increase my popularity.

Dear Diary,

I wrapped all the Hanukkah presents with aluminum foil because it looked pretty—<u>there was no other reason</u>. Since I finally had my own money, from work and baby-sitting, I wanted to buy good presents for my family. I bought my sister a Benetton sweater. I got my mom a peach bathrobe from Ralph

Lauren. And my Dad, I got him this vegetable chopper thing where you slide veggies over a piece of orange plastic that has blades in it. It sounds lame I guess. He's into chopping stuff. In total, I spent around $120. For once I wanted to get my parents good presents, especially since they always spend a lot on us.

You know, now that my family's pretty wealthy it's extremely difficult to buy my parents presents. When I was like six and we didn't have as much money, I used to make my mom a macaroni necklace and spray-paint it gold and she'd practically have convulsions over it. That shit just doesn't cut it anymore. Anyway, I was so excited to give them the presents yesterday. My mom looked at the silver box and turned it over and over. She started cracking up, which made me crack up to, although I had no clue what was so funny.

She goes, "This is aluminum foil, right?"

I go, "Yeah," kind of proud, like I'm creative or something. Except she gave my dad this look.

I go, "What?"

"How did we get such a cheap kid?" She said to my dad. She didn't say it in a mean way, more of a joking way. She's really hooked on people being cheap.

I said something about how I thought it *looked pretty*, it had nothing to do with price. I could tell she didn't believe me, so then I had to defend myself by saying that I wouldn't have spent almost half my money on gifts if I were cheap. As soon as I said that I was, like, the sorriest I ever felt in my life.

They opened the presents, the entire time going, "oh, you spent way to much" "you should save that money for yourself" and other stuff like that. Mom asked me where I bought her gift. She told me that she loved it to death, only needed to exchange it for a different color. Probably white. Everything in our house is white; I guess she wanted to blend in. My presents were about a hundred pairs of Guess jeans in every color. I also got a pair of sterling silver hoop earrings and this new Esprit wallet that's black. And the *St. Elmo's Fire* tape. And she even wrapped up some socks and other little things, to make it seem special.

I felt like such a LOSER!

Bye,

Sharone

Dear Diary,

This morning I was sitting in the kitchen, minding my own business and eating Froot Loops. I heard Mom in the other room, talking to Carol on the phone. She goes, "Danna painted me a picture and Sharone bought me a very nice bathrobe." That part was good. But then she goes, "Sharone wrapped the gift in aluminum foil. I'm telling you, I don't know how I got such a cheap kid!"

Oh my god, she said I'm cheap to Carol! The weird thing is, she said it proudly. As if she's *proud* that I'm cheap. I'm totally confused; does she want me to be cheap or not? Maybe parents who have money are proud when their kids are cheap, because it makes them seem humble? Back when my parents were poor they had to do everything in their power to seem like they had money, like iron underwear and stuff.

I know that one of our close family friends are also wealthy and love to spend, spend, spend. They think money grows on trees. It makes both my parents sick, how they are. So maybe my mom wants me to be kind of cheap, in a weird way.

Except whether she likes it or not, I don't want to be called cheap, especially when I'm not, and ESPECIALLY when I'm Jewish. When you're Jewish and cheap you're doomed. At school I have to act extra giving because I'm a Jew. Like if I'm in the food line to buy my Lorna Doones and tea in the morning, and some popular girl like Cindy McKlansky is in line in front of me, short of change or something, I *have* to give her money. I don't have a choice, it's a requirement.

If I were Irish-Catholic, like a lot of people in my town, I could blow her off completely. Cheap Jew is about the worst thing to be called in the entire world. The other worst thing in the entire world to be called is Rich Jew. I'm walking a very fine line here.

Bye,
Sharone

Dear Diary,

I made a big giant mistake. I drove dad's car to school today. In Social Studies in front of the whole class Mr. S goes, "Miss Katz, I saw your car—very nice. I wish I could have a Volvo someday too". OH MY GOD I'm like, totally freaking out! Now I'm a rich Jew! Cheap and rich. It's official! And everybody knows it.

I'm taking the bus from now on. This is terrible.
Bye.

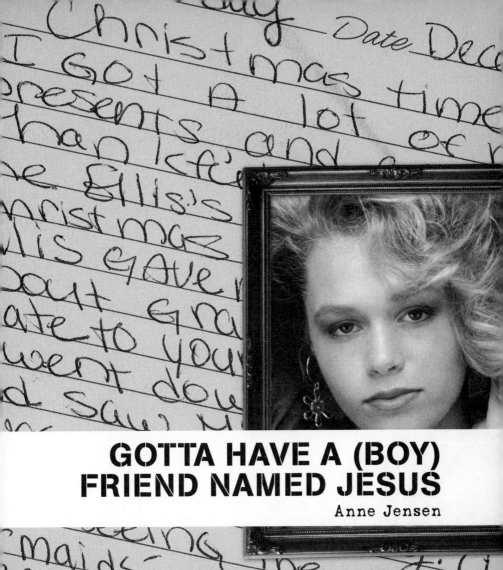
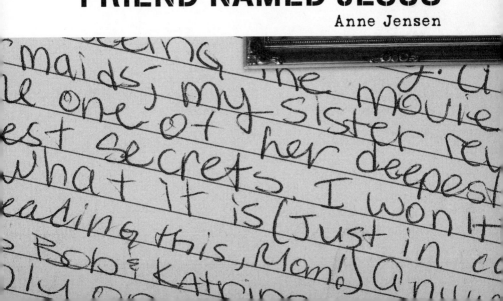

GOTTA HAVE A (BOY) FRIEND NAMED JESUS

Anne Jensen

These journal entries were written over the course of exactly one year—from Christmas of eighth grade to the Christmas of ninth grade.

This was an extremely difficult time for me because my parents had just gotten a divorce, I moved from junior high to high school, I had a numerous "best friends," I was becoming fat, and I was in love with every guy who merely said hi to me. There were no constants in my life. Relationships were rocky, and I was gaining weight faster than I could say "puberty."

So in a world where nothing was solid, I had to find my rock. And I did—in Jesus.

December 25, 1989

Today was Christmas. The first Christmas after my parents got a divorce. It was much different. It was fun!!! In the a.m., Dad came over and we opened presents and we had breakfast. My grandparents came, but not Aunt Kathy or Aunt Joyce. They are in a fight with my mom and my grandparents.

Thanks for everything, God,

Anne Jensen

January, 1990

Ever since I recommited my life to Christ on Saturday, I've been having such a good life. I kind of like this guy named Andy.

Later Love,

Anne Jensen

Febuary, 1990

Today is my 2 friends' birthday—Brandie and Steve. I love Steve so much and I don't know what to do. Laura is like taking him away from me, and now he likes her and hates me. At least he acts like it. He says he's still my friend. What a bunch of bologna! I still love him sooooo much, though! Tonight I'm going to Brandie's house. We've gotten to be great friends.

I still love Steve.

Love,

Anne Jensen

February, 1990

Today I did the papers and went collecting, then went to the bowling alley with Laura and her friend, Heather. We met Steve there. Laura is such a bitch! Because she used to think that he was a total jerk and now she likes Steve and is taking him away from me and now he barely even likes me as a friend and totally loves Laura. I love him so much and I don't know what to do.

Please help me God,

Anne Jensen

March, 1990

Today I went to the dentist. Pain! Major pain! I can't stop thinking about Steve! I love Steve so much!

Anne Jensen

April, 1990

Sorry I haven't written in a long time, but I've been in the process of moving on. I want to tell you what happened the other day. I was walking home from school and Laura said, "Look at that awesome guy" and I said, "That's Don." Anyways, to make a long story short, I walked home with him and he is so sweet. I can't believe it. And today I went to Subway (he works there, Josh does, too) and he fully talked to me like we were good friends. And Josh said "Hi" and asked how I was doing!!! God, I ask you to please let this lick repeat and let me become good friends with both Don and especially Josh.

Please God! Oh, and when I'm walking home from school tomorrow please let me walk with ~~Josh~~ Don because I have to talk him.

God please!

Anne Jensen

p.s. I'm mostly over Steve, but I've found the person I need—Josh or Don.

May, 1990

Today was different!! I really missed talking to Don! I also felt sad about it! Also because it seemed like Steve was mad at me! Oh well! It is sooooo hot! Yesterday it was about 109-104 degrees. Today Joanna and I started R.A.D. (Radical Active

Disciples). It's pretty fun! God, please let me walk home with Don tomorrow. It makes me feel really good to talk to him! God, you work through the both of us so please let this happen TOMORROW!!

These things I ask in YOUR SON'S NAME! Amen.

Thanks for today,

Anne Jensen

May, 1990

Two days ago I got my first kiss from my first boyfriend! His name is Peter!

Thanks God,

Anne Jensen

June, 1990

A lot has happened. Well, I dumped Peter a long time ago. I'm on Weight Watchers. Cool! Laura and I had a graduation party (because we graduated from the eighth grade) and her parents hired a live band! We were very surprised when they showed up at her front door.

Well, Laura is going out with Steve, so I guess him and me would've never worked out. Oh well!

love,

Anne Jensen

September, 1990

I'm going out with a senior and I'm a freshman!! He gave me my first FRENCH kiss a couple days ago, but I also like this guy named Pete L, but I think he likes Ari. Joanna is being a butthole tonight. She ignored me all night and then called and asked me what was wrong! Oh, my new boyfriend's name is Jamey.

Anne Jensen

September, 1990

Well, I broke up with Jamey a week ago! Oh well! He was too old anyways. I like someone else now. His name is Pete and he's a sophomore and we're friends now, but I guess that's all we will be.

Gotta plow!

Anne Jensen

October, 1990

I've tried (and am still trying) to get really involved with church. It's a really positive thing. I want to get really involved. I got my permit today. Watch out! I'll be on the road! I met this awesome guy Friday night! His name is Jack. Cool deal! Also, I sort of like John. He's rad! I'm listening to a Depeche Mode tape that Pete lent me today.

I'm confused. Maybe I don't like anyone, but *want to* like someone. Maybe I just like the *thought* of liking somebody. I wish somebody would like me. I like that thought. Gotta go now!

Bye bye,

Anne Jensen

November, 1990

Today is Friday. TGIF! Anyways, still no men in my life. Oh, well. I don't care. I'm more focused on <u>friendships</u> now. I don't really have any best friends, just a lot of friends. My new Drama teacher is totally cool. I better go.

Later days,

Anne Jensen

Tuesday, December 25, 1990

Christmas time again! I got a lot of nice presents and am very thankful. We went to the Ellis's house for Christmas dinner and Mr. Ellis gave me a big pep talk about grades and how they relate to your future life. So, I decided to wright down my good and bad points and think of ways to improve them, so here goes:

Good points:
1. My personality
2. I love God
3. I am kind to people I <u>first</u> meet

Bad points:
1. I talk about people behind their back
2. I'm short-tempered
3. I complain a lot
4. I let jealousy take me over
5. I don't try my hardest
6. I'm lazy
7. I'm critical of other people
8. I usually get my way

Well, when there are more bad points than good points I think we've got a problem on our hands. I need to improve these bad points, because I cannot bear to lose any of my friends. They are my life, I love them.

Lord, please help me to improve.

Anne Jensen

p.s. the reason I sign my name is because I like to!

TAXICAB
CONFESSIONAL

Blaise K

Like most teenage girls, I always wanted an epic kind of love. The kind of sweeping, forbidden, and everlasting romance where a gallant (and totally hot) swordsman rebels against the Montagues and the Capulets and snatches the eager and willing (and also totally hot) princess from her ivory tower.

Unfortunately, I did not live in Shakespeare's Verona.

I lived in Massachusetts.

I butted heads with my savagely divorced parents—a controlling, overprotective mother and a sensitive father who knew not how to handle his only adolescent daughter. I took whatever swordsman and chariot I could find (again, as long as the swordsman was hot and actually had a chariot, because that was important), preferring to fly blindly through my own not-so-enchanted reality.

May 25th, 1985

Dear Diary,

Today is Tuesday May 25th, 1985. I guess it's about 3 or 4 but, you see, I wouldn't really know because I'm stuck on the stairs again in a Time Out for a friggin' hour (but I'll get to that later).

I've always wanted to start a diary and I have tried many times but I can never keep up with them because, first of all, I'm lazy, second of all, I'm a procrastinator, and third of all, my whole life is like waiting to do something until a tomorrow that never comes! But now I've decided that I'm 12 now, and I've waited long enough and I think that your high school years are the hardest, and you have a lot of emotional problems during those years and a lot of the time I need someone to talk to—someone who will listen and understand and take some of the burden away just by doing those things. But this "thing" to confide in should not be just a "thing," it should be a friend too. Since a diary doesn't talk, hey, that might be the best friend you could ever have!

The reason why I have to sit on the stairs for an hour is because I was in a rage with my mother. But sitting here for an hour, I think it's worth it, because I hate her. I mean I REALLY hate her. I always have. When I tell my friends that I hate my mother they laugh and say, "I know, my parents are real bitches sometimes. I hate them too!" But it's not the same. All my friends get mad at their parents when they do something that they don't like and then they say that they hate them, but it's different with me. I don't think there's anything in this whole world that could make me not hate my mother. NOTHING.

But my father I love so much. The only thing is that when I show my report card or my progress reports and the grades are bad it makes me feel real cheap. They stink so much. Actually, they don't stink, they suck, and not only do they suck, they suck shit!

Welp, my hour is up. Now I have to drag myself to my

mother's room and sit there doing my homework for 2 1/2 hours and then I'll have to sit there while she checks my math. SCREW HER! Gotta go! I know we'll be great friends, Diary!

Love,

Blaise

October 1, 1987

Nothing much happened today. Oh, except my half-bro said he would buy 2 cases of Bud for us for Saturday night. Pretty awesome, eh? Talk to you later.

Oh my fucking God!

You are not going to believe what just happened! Remember Ian, the hot 20-year-old cabby? I saw him tonight! Oh my God, I can't even calm down. He was totally looking right into my eyes the whole time. I asked him if he was working tomorrow and he said he didn't know. I go, "Well, do you want to pick me up from school tomorrow?" To make a long story short I'm going to wait for him until 4:30 and if he doesn't show up I'll just leave.

But get this: He goes, "So do you have a phone number for me?" I shit the biggest fucking bricks you ever saw! Oh my fucking god! I can't believe it! This is the most gorgeous guy I've ever met! What if he doesn't call me? What if my dad answers the phone? FUCK! FUCK! FUCK!

October 2, 1987

What I thought was going to be a pretty good day turned out to be a sack of the biggest shit pile you've ever seen.

October 7, 1987

Me and Tess and Kate got to Harvard Square at 5:30. We were meeting Ian in The Pit. I spotted him right away behind the ramp near the skaters and the punks and the skinheads. He was wearing army pants and a blue USMC sweatshirt. We sat down and had a few cigarettes. I inhaled.

We met Ian's friends and hung out until 8:30. The guys went to the liquor store. They came back with who knows how much beer, two bottles of tequila and a whole bunch of lemons. Then it was off to The Squat. Kate didn't drink a whole beer because she felt ill and Tess got shit-faced faster than you could play "Stairway To Heaven." I was buzzed too. Maybe, really, for the first time. Ian was out of it. Everyone was drunk.

Oz tried to molest me and Adam tried to molest Tess and Ian was nowhere to be found. Suddenly there he was and we were alone on the bed. I wouldn't. I couldn't. He was way too drunk, too out of it, too out of control. He still thinks I'm 17 (DUH. Maybe because that's what I told him?!) And I DID NOT tell him I'm a virgin yet. We went downstairs and he disappeared. Adam started trying to kiss me and the camera that was in the pocket of my jacket was gone.

October 14, 1987

I swear to god, this week is going by sooooo slow.

I can't believe I haven't written in one whole week! Last Wednesday Ian pulled up to the front of my house and YOU KNOW I was practically waiting at the door! I ran out to his car and asked him what he was doing here?! He said that he had to go pick up somebody at The Chestnut Hill Mall and he stopped by for a couple of minutes.

Then I told him I was so mad at him because I was waiting and waiting at school for him and he never showed. (What happened was the dispatcher knew that Ian and I knew each other and he bitched Ian out ["NO SOCIAL CALLS!"])

Ian looked great. He's really beautiful.

"So what are you doing this weekend," he asked. I told him that I was going to Amy's keg party.

"Can I come?"

I told him he could but that he might think it was lame because her parents might be there and everyone there wouldn't be old as he is (20).

"Can you get out right now?"

I told him I couldn't because my dad would shit.

For a second, Ian sort of looked away towards my driveway and said, "Well, I gotta go. I have to go pick up this person at the Mall . . ." Then, still looking towards the driveway, he lifted up his chin, made a bit of a face and I knew that he wanted to kiss me. He looked back over at me and put his arm through the window and around my waist. I leaned over. And we kissed. First one little kiss. Then another little kiss. Then another. Then he started to open his mouth and I could feel his soft, gentle hand going up and down on my back. We were really making out. And then his tongue. Then there was another little kiss. And another. And another. And we pulled away.

"Well, I've gotta go," he says. "Are you sure you can't get out? Meet me up at the Mall." I couldn't. There was no way. "Can you get out later?" he asks.

"No, I can't. My dad will shit." We kissed again. I wanted to touch the side of his face like I usually do to guys when

I'm kissing them, but it was kind of difficult because he was sitting in the car and I was leaning outside of it by his door so I wouldn't have been abl—

OH MY GODD!!!! Ian was just here! Just now! He just came by as I was writing that last sentence! Holy shit! Okay, calm down. Omigod—now I have even MORE to tell you! Okay, anyway. As I was saying we talked some more and then he left and then I ran into the house and what did I do? I SHIT BRICKS!!

OMG now Rich just called me. This night is crazy! He's this guy I met on Tuesday. I was uptown talking to Tess on a pay phone and this guy with a gorgeous girl in the front seat pulled up in a red Pontiac Fiero. At first I thought he was a total scum trying to pick me up with his girlfriend in the car. She even waved to me but then I found out that she was his sister Monica and she was a dancer in "Dirty Dancing." She was really nice. Anyway, he certainly wasn't "gorgeous." He's 21 and he knows I'm 15. He called me and asked when we could get together. I'm undecided.

October 18, 1987
Sixth period study hall.

. . . Just another shit day in the life of a late night teenager forced to play in the day.

I've got detention tomorrow from 3:15 to 4:30 for talking on the pay phone to Ian when it wasn't break or lunchtime. The ironic thing about it was the conversation between Ian and me sucked the big one and it wasn't even worth serving detention for.

October 22nd, 1987

I got into the most massive fight with Steve this morning over the phone. He is such a fucking little shit and he's NOT coming to the party this weekend. The only bad part about that is now we don't have wine coolers, not to mention a keg, but I'm just praying that Phil can help us out . . . OH RUSH!!! "Carrie" by Europe just came on Z94!

Okay. I'm sorry. I just had to hear that song. It's such an awesome song. I think it's like number five or something. The lead singer of the band who sings it, is just amazing. He's got one of those voices that just gets to me, y'know? His name is Joey Tempest and when I saw him in the video I almost shit. He just gets so into the song and I can hear that in his voice over the radio. God, I just get so caught up in music it's not even funny.

Thursday, October 24, 1987

Today at school it was our last day to practice "I Heard It Through The Grapevine" for the lip sync contest during assembly tomorrow. I skipped aerobics and stayed after school with Amy to practice with everyone else. I got home at 7:30. Around 9:00 there was a faint sound of a horn outside. I was sitting on my bed and my Dad was upstairs. I didn't think the horn was Ian at all, or anybody, but something made me get up and go to the window. I saw two taillights driving away. I ran to the hall and opened the front door and saw a cab turning around. I knew it was Ian. He came back down the street and pulled up in front of my house.

My dad saw me go outside and saw me talking to him. I

couldn't avoid it. When I came inside my dad walked into my room. "So who's this guy in the taxi cab?"

I told him he was a friend of mine who worked for Yellow Cab.

"How old is he?"

"Oh. Um, 17 . . .."

"He's 17 and works for a cab company??"

YES! I'VE KNOWN HIM FOR YEARS! LEAVE ME ALONE!

Later, when I was talking to Amy on the phone my dad came in and said, "Does this guy know that you're 15?"

I told him yes and he's only 17. What a joke. I need a smoke.

October 26, 1987

Guess what? I snuck out of my house last night and Ian picked me up in the yellow cab. What a BABE! Climbing in and out of my window is such a rush. Watch my dad find my diary and read this!

I had so much fun with Ian last night. I met him up by Dr. Kaplan's office around the corner from the nursing home, and we parked up near the depot on Centre Street by the bank. We went to third. Fuck, he knows exactly what he's doing and more! We were in the cab for about a half an hour and then he got a call on the radio. We went to go pick up this lady who was going to the airport and then we just cruised around Boston and Cambridge.

At 11:37 he dropped me off at the top of my street. We talked and we kissed and talked some more. He gave me a sweet kiss goodnight and then I climbed back through my window and shit bricks. It was as if I had never even left.

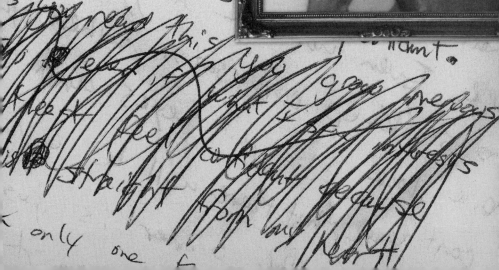

PROBLEM CHILD

Neil Katcher

When I was a teenager, I spent half of my time yearning for a girlfriend and the other half devising ways to avoid asking a girl out. Not only was I a total coward, but I was also incredibly counterproductive. All I had to do was ask a girl out. I couldn't do it. My refusal to face rejection head-on left me *extremely* bitter.

I didn't blame anyone in particular for my shortcomings. I blamed the entire world . . . through poetry.

I wrote this poem when my senior year crush went to prom with someone else.

"Prom Is a Fantasy"

Prom is a fantasy.
A fantasy that went out with all the others
at the end of the 50's.
You should go to Prom, though.
You should also go to college
Get a well-paying job
Get married
Have at least two children
Live in a white house with a white picket fence
And have a dog named Spot.

This used to be called the American <u>Dream</u>.
But a dream is exactly what this is.

Why should we subject ourselves to this cruel and
unjustified
Myth? . . .
The American <u>Reality</u> is that everyone has different
tastes and styles.
And for this reason, we must each set our own
goals.
If one's reason to go to the prom
Is just so they can say they went . . .

Maybe they should look at how much
They are letting society dictate their actions.

ADULT ME SAYS

So after all that . . . I ended up going to prom . . . with
a blind date. The experience left me even more bitter. I
locked myself in my bedroom, dug way down, and wrote an
even more bitter poem.

"Untitled"
Death to the Tormentors!
Glance over to the persecutors and then release your
fury.

The beginning of the end.

The damnation of love.

The hell fires of paradise reign free as the good take the night like raging packs of wolves.

Hate and destruction kills all evil.

They play that grand old symphony with pleasure as the listeners shreak in pain.

Cover the secrets and let be known the obvious for the first time.

The omnipotent coward controls the tired puppets.

Entertain us and laugh at yourselves.

Time has no place in the eternal flame.

Venim shall spew from the angels hearts.

Poison soothes the soul.

Freedom rings loudly inside the guts of the oppressors and curses the downtrodden.

It will all happen in the past.

Look into the eyes of the Blind one and it will guide you.

Those winners lost the war and those losers are dead.

So go home . . . and wait for the apocalypse

Of the world.

ADULT ME SAYS

Frustrated, I devised the perfect scheme to find true love. All I had to do was find a girl with *bigger* problems than mine. After all, I was merely failing school, my sister was gay, and my father had cancer. But where could I find a girl who could possibly top all that? Study hall.

Friday, June 16th

I love Melissa Paloma. Melissa was molested. I found out two days ago in study hall.

It is *all* I can think about. Her parents are divorced. Her father cheated on her mother. She tried to commit suicide.

I love her.

Melissa does not know I love her. She's moving to Cincinnati.

ADULT ME SAYS

Even that failed. So I finally decided to face my fears and do something I had never done before: ask a girl out. I wrote a love letter to a virtual stranger who picked up trash at the state park. I wasn't just attracted to girls with problems anymore. I was attracted to girls with the *potential* for problems.

Andrea,

It is time I bare my soul to you. The first time I looked into your eyes I knew then what I know now and that is I see more than the others see.

Every time our eyes meet my heart skips a beat, then quickly grows warmer and warmer and that feeling of warmth reaches up into my throat and down into the depths of my stomach.

This is only the tip of the iceberg of my feelings for you but do not fear because I will respect and treat you like the Queen of England.

Andrea, the light of love is on the horizon, so do not keep us in the dark.

This light will be seen by all, because it will shine from our hearts and out through our eyes so take a chance because the future is as bright as the awaiting horizon and let me gaze into your beautiful eyes for more than just a moment at a time.

ADULT ME SAYS

Unfortunately, when I approached Andrea with the love letter, she was holding hands with a guy twice my size. I went home with the note still in my pocket, walked into my bedroom, and wrote this final note of defeat on the back.

It is the middle of the day but I choose to sit in darkness. My fear had done me in before I had a chance to do it in. Standing where I had prayed to be was a statue made by Michelangelo's hands. She held him, and he lead her away into the sunset.

The words in my pocket felt like the meaningless rambling of an idiot as it sat unknown to all except the conquered one. The enemy of the messenger is none other than his messages for they required true feeling but now they are the direct permanent records of his descent into anguish.

AN OLYMPIC-SIZE LOVE

Christina Kerby

The 1988 Summer Olympics made quite an impact on me during fifth grade. I went back to school that fall swollen with national pride and athletic fervor and wanted to share my Olympic spirit with the rest of the world.

I blasted Whitney Houston's "One Moment in Time" from my stereo at all hours of the day and night and scrawled the lyrics on binders, on my desk, on my sneakers, etc. As evidenced by my poetry, visions of gold medals danced in my head.

Unfortunately, visions of a certain medal-winning high diver danced across the pages of my journal.

September 28, 1988

Dear Journal,

I feel kind of like a sausage right now, so I'll just twist my pen for a while. Do you know how cute Greg Louganis is? Well, for starters, he's an excellent diver—wait, let me put it in the way my teacher would want it.

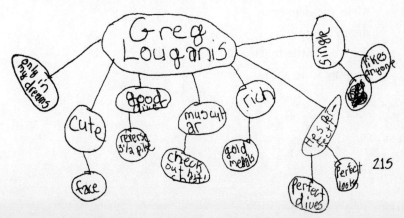

September 29, 1988

People I Heart (love)

Greg Louganis

James Anderson

Davy Jones

Danny Huddleston

Twinkie [my hamster]

Blackie [my guinea pig]

Any thing or person which I call *darling*

September 30, 1988

Dear Journal,

    I'm not really in the mood for journal writing but look, I'm writing. I can't think of any more things about Greg Louganis to tell you and I'm not in the mood to tell you about the dream I had about him.

October 4, 1988

The Olympics

    The Olympics are over
    but the spirit won't die.
    When the torch was extinguished,
    I thought I would cry.
    All of the dancers,
    their elegant feet,
    dancing to the music,
    keeping time with the beat.

I know I'll have to wait,
Four more years.
The thought of waiting,
Produces tears.

Maybe when the Olympics,
Come again,
I'll be participating
With them.
"Them" is the athletes,
so talented and strong.
Maybe four more years
Won't be so long.

October 5, 1988

My Dream

My dream is to share
The glory and joy
Of being in the Olympics
With every girl and every boy.

To bounce off the high dive,
Into the pool.
To run a race
Will make me look cool.

To ride on a horse,
Swim a race of my kind,

To win a gold medal,
Is a wonderful find.

I LOVE EVERYBODY!!!

ADULT ME SAYS

Here are a few snippets from my sixth-grade journal.
No wonder I considered my journal my only "true"
friend . . .

September 24, 1989

Dear Journal,

I've just finished writing about best friends. It was sort of
hard, thinking about Jessica. I'm glad that now I have Jennifer
as a best friend. She fits my description perfectly. I wish that
Jessica would.

You know how I used to think that I'd never get any "hairs?"
Well, I've got some! They're really light and hard to see, but my
longest one is about like this ____ (at least, that's what I've seen
so far!).

I don't feel like writing right now (no offense), but I have
to. Well, I guess I've written enough.

Bye!

Christina

November 1, 1989

Dear Journal,

Hi! I've missed you! Sorry I haven't written in such a long time. I don't want to bore you with my problems with Jessica, but I'm afraid that I have to. Last night was Halloween, and I went trick-or-treating with Jessica. It was sort of fun, and I got lots of candy, but I just wanted to get away from her after a while. That girl is SO immature! When it comes down to physical maturity, though, Jessica is tops.

She is really developed, and has a meadow of pubic hair!

November 5, 1989

Dear Journal,

Last year, my favorite expression was, "I feel like a sausage right now." This year, I've decided on "Goodness gracious, great balls of meatloaf!" You can't just think of a good expression, it comes to you when you are ready. That's how I came up with meatloaf.

ADULT ME SAYS

And finally, just to show how excited I was about everything in the world at that time, here's a rap I wrote—about sausages.

The Sausage Rap
  I'm a sausage, you're a sausage, everyone's a sausage!
  Brown and crispy, nice and hot

I'm a sausage and you're not!
I feel greasy, you feel dry
Have a sausage, then say "Hi!"
To go with your sausage, bacon and eggs.
You're having cereal? Hey, use your head!

"YEA!"

Sausage can be lean,
Sausage can be mean.
Sausage can be fat,
Sausage can be flat.
What do you think of that?

HORUS HEARS A HO

Jennifer Kirmse

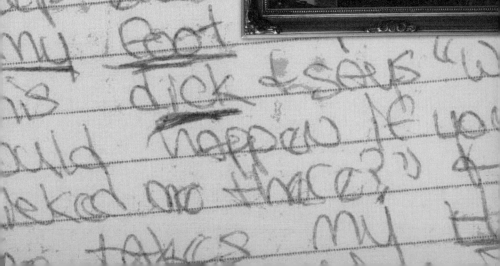

Diary

I knew a boy named Horus in eighth grade. He had sandy blond hair, green eyes, and a cute smile—the all-American boy-next-door type. He actually *was* the boy next door, since we lived in the same condo complex. This made breaking into his house a breeze.

Often my best friend, Kristin, and I would go there and decorate his room with rose petals and write "We love you, Horus" on his mirror with lipstick. We snatched a Polaroid of him wearing nothing but a towel. I believe we also stole some underpants.

We were obsessed with sex. While Kristin was actually seeing some action, I was merely *imagining* what it might be like. I don't think I ever considered what I might *do* when faced with the opportunity myself.

But rather than admitting my hurdle to getting a guy was *me*, I chose to jealously blame everything on the ever-perky, popular, and, worst of all, *nice* Sunshine. Everyone wanted to sit next to her at lunch or hang out at her place after school. All the guys liked her.

3/28/84

Karen seems totally pissed and I don't even know why. Yesterday she was too! Whatever. Her and Sunshine are totally buddy-buddy now.

4/4/84

I fucking don't even believe what's going on! Karen said that she, Christine, Sunshine, Horus and Scot were all spending the night Friday at Scot's house and getting stoned. I'm seriously contemplating suicide. If Karen got Horus, I'd die. OH SHIT. Sunshine has ruined all of my life. She is now stealing and using Karen! FUCK! I hate SUNSHINE and LIFE!

4/6/84

Thank God that Friday thing has gotten all fucked up—Horus isn't going anymore. Told Karen that Sunshine said that she and Horus would probably get together. Life sucks since Sept.

4/9/84

11:00 PM. Shit. 7 hours of sleep. Great. Report in English due. Freezing. Karen. Horus. I HATE SUNSHINE.

4/13/84

Asked Amy to come skiing but she doesn't know how. Mom is uncomfortable with this. I'm gonna die! Still ill.

I will always hate Sunshine. Devil from hell. Always. Forever.

4/20/84

Power went off in Math. Weird spot on my hand. Sunshine is staying with Karen till like Wed. Sucks. Never gonna see her. I'm gonna go see *Pretty in Pink* w/ Amy next Friday. I HATE SUNSHINE. DEVIL-WORSHIPER.

5/8/84

I'm going to Howard Jones June 8! COOL! I HATE SUNSHINE, I LOVE KAREN. Kristin told Horus about the underwear we stole so I gave them to him at school and they turned out to be Scot's! I was inspecting them too! Louis knows we stole them and so does the whole school!

5/13/84

Mom keeps nagging. I thought I liked Horus and then he turned out to be a dick! He needed a protractor for math and he came in and we talked and I showed him my graduation dress and told him we broke in [his home] today. Later, I asked if he wanted to come over and that he had to make up his mind in 30 minutes. I'm annoyed. I wanted to fuck him BAD. And mom was at a meeting. He wanted to stay home and make a fucking toy airplane instead!

5/20/84

Sick. Christine, Kristin and Karen came over after school and surprised me. Broke into Horus's and his stepmom was there! Shit! Long story. Later we talked and he said that Scot hates me cuz I hate him and Horus asked who I liked and I didn't say. I asked him and he said Sunshine, a little.

5/22/84

I went over to Horus's after school and he said he had to change so I said "I'll join you." I would have, too! Richard Gere is so fine! Do I like Horus? His brother was saying "You looove Jennifer, right Horus?" and Horus is all "Yes."

He was just joking unfortunately.

5/25/84

Howard Jones is so soon! God I was so horny tonight. I feel so bad that I've never done anything! Horus was giving me a massage twice and I gave him one. It was FUN! His skin is so soft! Sometime, when Horus says something nice, I want to kiss him!

5/29/84

I broke my tailbone. Very painful. Fell on my ass at lunch while playing softball! Horus came over and we had a party with his condom and my sponge. Told Horus that I like him and he said he wasn't sure cause I seemed real mad. I WAS! Told him that "One More Night", "Crazy For You" and "Against All Odds" remind me of him.

"One more night, give me just one more night, one more night cause I can't wait forever"

6/6/84

I feel SO strange. Like sexually aroused or something! I was swimming with Horus for like an hour and he kept trying to tickle my sides and I was so scared that he was going to get my tit! Then he was trying to learn how to do the back somersault and he tickled me when I wasn't looking. Then we were in the deep end and he takes <u>my foot</u> and puts it on <u>his dick</u> and says "What would happen if you kicked me there?" and then he takes my <u>HAND</u> and starts pulling it and I'm all "NOT EVEN!" I was so fuckin scared! SHIT! He kept feeling his dick—he must have had a boner. I was so scared!

Was he making a pass? DOUBTFUL.

6/8/84

WHY ME? I don't know! This is absolutely the *last* time Horus pisses me off. I'm sorry, he just does it and I guess I overreact. SHIT. I HATE HIM.

Why? Picnic Fri. Get bikini wax! I called and he didn't say "Hold on." He just left me there w/ his brother to annoy me. I know it!

Fuck. Revenge.

But how?

Think.

Fuck you, Horus.

THE CHALLENGER SONG
Krista Lanphear and Keleigh Lanphear

In 1986, when we were in sixth grade, we and some other girls in our class formed a club called the Material Girls. We met every day at recess to discuss fashion, talk about boys, and, of course, choreograph awesome dance routines.

That same year, a horrible American tragedy took place, and the Material Girls decided it was time to stop being so materialistic. So we wrote a song about the tragedy with the high (and delusional) hopes of *healing the nation*. We thought it was going to be the next "We Are the World." But it wasn't even "Hands Across America."

We are so "proud" to finally present this song to the world.

The Challenger Song

I'm sorry to say
I'll make it short and subtle
But our fellow Americans
Have vanished in the Shuttle

The Challenger

The Shuttle went up
But it didn't come down

I'm sorry to say
There was no one to be found
But don't worry they are safe
In heaven right now

The Challenger Crew

Don't try to hide
Your feelings inside
You should have a lot of pride
For the brave astronauts

Of the Challenger

They found a piece
In the Atlantic Ocean
But it's not
Much of a potion
To make you feel better
About the Challenger

(GUITAR SOLO)

Don't try to hide
Your feelings inside
You should have a lot of pride
For the brave astronauts

Of the Challenger . . .

(ALL SING)

I'm sorry to say
I'll make it short and subtle
But our fellow Americans
Have vanished in the Shuttle

The Challenger

STALKING MANDY
MOSKOVITZ

Scott Lifton

The following is from journal I wrote when I was fifteen. At that age, I was a little behind in my maturity. My friends were beginning to have sex, and I was not.

As a result, I had a *lot* of pent-up sexual frustration that I aimed toward the most popular girl in school, who, coincidentally, was also the most developed. So I decided one day to take the next step . . . not toward asking her out or anything, but toward *stalking* her.

9/16/91

IMPORTANT DAY IN HISTORY! Billy got laid today with his girlfriend Karen. He said it was under the covers with only shirts on (and a condom) for 3 minutes. Wow. He's lucky he found a girl like that. They both love each other. I hope I'll get that.

9/17/91

Mandy Moskovitz!! I have liked this girl since the 8th grade. She has long blonde hair, green eyes, she's tan, huge tits, nice ass and great body. She is the embodiment of human perfection . . . The one thing I used to look forward to all day long was seeing her, looking at her. Seeing what she was wearing. Right now . . . I'm making a dossier on her classes, periods, address, and telephone number.

9/18/91

YOM KIPPUR. Well I didn't eat until a little after five. I was basically pretty bored until Eric and Don came over and we watched *New Jack City*. I gave it an 8 1/2.

I'm worried about school tomorrow. Well, at least I get to see Mandy. I want this girl so much. She's unfortunately one of the most popular girls in the grade and I think she's going out with a college guy. I recently wrote a song about her, "There's **a** Piece of You in My Heart".

I would do almost anything for her. I would even just like a picture of her (especially in a bikini). I think of sneaking into her house. I do know where she lives.

9/20/91

I drove Billy to Eric's house and then the theater where we saw *Necessary Roughness*, 8 1/2. I'm tired. Mandy!!!! Sorry I had to let that out. Her picture in last year's yearbook is so good. Between Mandy and Michelle Pfeiffer I don't know who rates first.

10/5/91 Saturday

Traci's Sweet 16: I was in my fly Cavaricci outfit. I danced . . . I danced very well. I played this contest with Laura where she put a roll of toilet paper between her legs and I put a stick between mine and I had to stick it in the hole forwards and backwards. I won.

I won a paddle with ball and string.

10/7/91

In science, I heard someone who's good friends with Mandy

238

talking with these girls and he said Mandy had sex last year. I wanted to be her first. All of a sudden, I got an image of her having sex. AND WITH SOMEONE ELSE. I couldn't think through my social studies test. She's so hot and has such a great body.

10/8/91

In social psychology we had to find one event that impacted our whole lives. I couldn't think of anything. The girl I got paired up with had her father die.

In study hall, Billy found a book that showed kangaroos and giraffes having sex—from behind!

10/10/91

Mandy is so beautiful. I really want pictures of her bad . . . How bad you ask? Well today I purchased this little mini camera/film thing for $10. It has 24 pictures and it's small and silent. I'm so excited. When I'm going down the hall—snap! I can't wait to get her, her ass, and her tits on film. Yes!!!

10/14/91

I can't wait to get my pictures. Not only of Mandy. Lea has the nicest ass. She was up at the board in Italian for 20 minutes with tight jeans.

Billy was on acid today. He called to tell me how he pissed his bed.

10/19/91

I was basically bored until Eric and Mike came over and we saw the *Book of Love*. I think it was pretty good—81/2. It was one of those movies where it was exactly how you expect it to be. Meanwhile, I was thinking *Frankie and Johnny* was a fucking great movie. There are so many things I love about it, 91/2!

10/21/91

Oh yeah, that camera was well worth its 10 dollars. I got two pictures of Mandy in front of me. She was wearing a jersey and white spandex.

Eric's birthday is tomorrow and I was going to get him a cool poster but they didn't have it. I think I'll get him a crossbow and a dragon.

10/24/91

Oh my god! I just made a green shit. I've never made a green shit before.

I got all of 2 pictures today. When I was finally gonna get one of Mandy, she was looking at me kind of pissed I think. She's not stupid. Maybe she realizes I see her like 200 times a day. I think I should be more careful.

10/27/91 Tuesday

Hey I'm worried . . . I owe so much to so many tape clubs.

Eric and Billy came over. We watched *Navy Seals*. 81/2. Oh God, Mandy looked good today. She wore a black spandex top tucked in. I missed the perfect picture a few times by a second.

11/5/91

Well the film has just been dropped off and we're waiting for the results. I used a fake name.

Later that day . . .

DAMN! I got the fuckin' pictures!!!! And none came out.

I have two, one of a tree, and one which I can't tell! I knew it!

I'm not going to give up though. No way. I'll think of something. Mandy!! I want a picture of her so badly. I seriously consider breaking into her house. I gotta sleep this off.

BULLY PULPIT

Gabriel Lopez

I was a very mean kid growing up in San Juan, Puerto Rico. I would write cruel songs about people and then force them to listen to me sing until they cried. Below are two of these songs, followed by their English translation.

This first song is one I wrote about a fat kid named Alberto in the summer of 1987 when I was thirteen. The tune is borrowed from a popular eighties song by Bon Jovi.

Bola De Queso
(to the tune of Bon Jovi's "Living on a Prayer")

Yo Tengo un Amigo que se llama Alberto.
Y Le Dicen "Bola De Queso," "Bola De Queso"

I have a friend and his name his Albert.
And we call him the cheese ball, the cheese ball.

El Tiene una amiga que se llama Nori
Y ella le dice que no, que no

He has a friend, and her name is Nori
And she says no to him, she says no to him.

Pero el es redondito y no puede hacer na
El tiene una barriga que parece una bolita
Y por eso ella le dice que no y le dice que no

But he is rounded and he can't do anything about it
He has a belly that looks like a ball
And that's why she said no, why she said no

Oh, El es Gordito
Oh, Oh, Bola de Quesito
El tiene unas clase de cuajitos
Oh, oh bola de quesito.

Oh, He's a little fatty.
Oh, oh the Cheese Ball.
He has big ear lobes
Oh, Oh, the Cheese Ball.

ADULT ME SAYS

The next song is about a strange kid in my neighborhood who hung out with my friend Teo. I don't think I ever knew his name. I just called him the Monkey. This is a tune that I wrote in the winter of 1988 when I was fourteen. And if you think it doesn't make any sense in English, it makes even less sense in Spanish.

Mi Cimi or "My Monkey"

El es feo, el es feo.
Y Del susto yo me meo.

He is ugly, he is ugly.
I'm so scared I pissed myself.

Me tiro un peo, me tiro un peo
Yo tocara en la casa de teo
No es Edgardo, no es Leonardo, no es Jimmy, es mi
Cimi

I fart, I fart.
I knock on Teo's house
He's not Edgar, he's not Leonard, He's not Jimmy, he's my
monkey.

Si lo vas a conocer, se que tu vas a corer
Puñeta, Puñeta, me cago en tu madre

If you meet him in the future, I know you're going to run away
Masturbate, Maturbate, I shit on your mother.

A ti no hay perro que te ladre
Estas carbon, te pareces a Joe y tambien te pareces a bob

There's no dog that's going to bark at you.
You are a bastard, you look like Joe and also, you look like
bob.

TWISTED SISTER

Jennifer McDonnell

SISTER ♥ ANDY

In January of 1989, I was twelve years old, and my older sister, Kristen, had recently returned home for her first semester's winter break of college. My eighteen-year-old sister's lifestyle fascinated me.

I wanted to be just like her. Unfortunately she wanted absolutely nothing to do with me. So I resorted to snooping. I'd go into her bedroom when she wasn't around, try on her clothes, listen to her music, and read her personal letters.

One day I came across a note that her boyfriend, Andy, had written to her. As it turned out, Kristen had started smoking while at college and my mom must have found out. I assume that my mom had a major freak-out on Kristen, and this note was Andy's way of consoling my sister. The most important thing to realize is that there was a very sarcastic edge to Andy's note that went completely over my twelve-year-old head.

I took everything he wrote at face value and walked away believing my sister was throwing her entire life away to become a crack whore. What follows is my overly concerned response to save her.

Monday, January 2, 1989
This news I'm gonna be writing isn't funny, and I swear to

251

God, if anyone is reading this you better shut it now, cuz this is NONE of your business! Of course, it seems as if everyone in my family but me know about it. See this is what happened.

I answered Kristen's phone [when] some guy named Sterling called. I was trying to find something to write it on, some paper she didn't need. So I saw a yellow paper on her desk folded in fourths, so I picked it up, to see if it was trash that I could write on. I opened it up and saw it was a letter to her from [her boyfriend] Andy. I was gonna put it down cuz you know, it's personal, but something in my head told me not to. This probably took only 5, 10 seconds. So for some stupid reason I read it. I say stupid, cuz I wish I hadn't, I would have been better off not knowing.

In the beginning it was just some shit about how Andy had liked it here over Christmas and how our family was real nice to him, and he wished he didn't have to leave. Real boring stuff. But then came the shock. And I'm trying to quote as best I can:

"So now that you smoke and you're cool . . ."

Wait! Hold on! What the hell? She *smokes*? Since when?

I read it over 3 times. Yep! It said it alright! She smokes cigarettes. Oh My God. I mean, I knew Andy smoked, but Kristen? But wait, I hadn't finished the letter. Right after it had said "and now you're cool" it went on to say, and once again I'm quoting as best I can:

" . . .maybe some time we could get together and do some crack or heroine. Sorry your mom got all freaked when she found out, but you gotta let her know you're growin' up and you have your own life to live."

WHAT THE FUCK? SHE DOES COKE? HEROINE? MOM KNOWS? DAMN RIGHT SHE GOT ALL FREAKED! IF I WAS HER I WOULD OF SLAPPED THE BITCH! MAYBE SHE DID! I HOPE SO!

Oh! She's growing up, huh? Oh right! All big "cool" people do pot, right? It means you're "in," it means you're "cool." It means you are a GODDAMNED FUCKED UP PERSON!

And I cried when I found out, just like I am now! It hurts to know she could be so stupid. I used to look up to her, now I hope she DIES! How could she fuck up her life like that?

I kinda hope she does keep on smoking that shit, then she can shrivel up and die! And it would be just like committing suicide, cuz she brought it on by herself. I hope her lungs decay, and her heart gives out, and she just dies feeling "good." Getting "stoked" she calls it.

WELL, FUCK YOU BITCH! GET STOKED. JUST GO AHEAD AND DIE! SEE IF I CARE! SHIT YOU'RE ONE GODDAMNED FUCKED UP KIND OF PERSON! AND I WISH YOU WEREN'T MY SISTER! WHAT DO I CARE IF YOU'RE KILLING YOURSELF? HUH? ANSWER ME!!!

If I don't care then why am I crying? I hate her so much, yet I feel kinda sorry for her cuz she used to be so nice, even if we did fight, I just always liked showing off her picture.

WELL NO MORE! I feel sorry for her cuz she's killing herself and no one seems to care! I mean what can my mom do about it? Or my dad? She's 18, she's "grown up." Well, fuck that! And her friends think it's "cool." Well, they can rot in hell with her! See if I give a shit!

FUCK THEM!

FUCK HER!

FUCK ALL OF THEM!

Later today, 3:40 pm, January 2, 1989

I've had about 2 or 3 hours to think. I read somewhere, at sometime, I don't know where, it said "Somewhere, in everyone's heart there is a child, [and] at one point or another that part of the heart dies. Some at 13, some at 18, some at 7, but everyone's child dies. It doesn't feel good, but you know that you've grown up and you'll never get that feeling again."

Well, I think Kristen's child just died. She's grown up by taking drugs. I still think she's fucked for doing it, but I think it's her decision and I can't change it. I think there is a part in my heart that just died too.

That piece right there died. Half is still there though. I'll always love her but the other half's gone. It's been tampered with, it's been fucked. I miss that piece. God! I can't stop crying!

Kristen,

You're fucked up! If you tell mom I said that I don't care because I think she feels the same.

I just wanted you to know, you are killing yourself. One day I'll be woken up by mom or dad at 3 in the morning, "Jennifer . . ." her eyes will be swollen by tears, "Jennifer, Kristen is dead." I'll start crying. She'll sit down by the side of my bed and say, "The coroner says it was drug addiction. She just had too much."

And then I'll think to myself, "She did it to herself. Maybe I shouldn't get sick over it all. It's her own fault, let her float away. See if I care. I warned her." And then I'll start crying once more.

So once again, I just wanted to say, you're fucked.

From,

Your Sister

Jennifer

MY FIRST

Rylan Morrison

I am impatient. I was impatient for true love by junior high. I hadn't figured out what it was I wanted with someone else exactly, but I had set my heart on Paul.

My life revolved around the tracking and logging of the possibility of maybe, just maybe, being close enough to him to see if it was real . . . or imagined.

10/13/92 9:22 pm
This is my last night alive being a child. Tomorrow at 11:00 I will be a full-blown teen!

10/19/92 9:13 pm
Today Paul Demartino and I actually had conversations and walked together as friends. I like him. I declare Margaret to be my best friend. She doesn't have to know.

10/27/92 6:48 am
I am still in love with Paul. Nothing new! But I'm a nun for Halloween!

10/27/92 8:31 pm
Today I "heard" that Paul is spreading a rumor that I'm going out with him!!!!

Does this mean he likes me??? In Technology he didn't say anything!

10/28/92

I'm begging to say something! I feel for Paul. I think he feels for me. He's perfect. I don't care if a lot of people can't stand him. I love Paul.

10/30/92

Yesterday Paul left the Technology room (probably in trouble) but anyways he said, "I love you Rylan!" I wonder if he meant it?? I love him! Let's see how today goes.

11/3/92 9:06 pm

Today was a weird day. In Spanish Paul and I found ourselves staring at each other and we did talk. We also got close by playing a little game of gentle push and shove.

11/4/92 9:10 pm

Today Tiffany asked Paul out for me, but I didn't ask her to! She just assumed. Well he didn't say anything. But HE defined ME as a skater girl! That's my goal!! Can you believe it?!

11/8/92

I just wrote down all the pros and cons of Paul and there's 18 pros and only 3 cons (They don't really matter) and all the pros are good, duh. He's all that I think of and all that I write and talk to my friends about.

11/9/92

Well I'm in love with Paul and I hope he says yes, I know he will, ok I don't. But I wouldn't understand why he wouldn't! I mean almost every day I write stuff about how he shows interest!! And he's really my type so hopefully I'll have a boyfriend!!!!!

11/11/92 8:35 pm

I got Paul's answer, actually Margaret did! He said I've thought about it and he just wants to be friends. I have mixed feelings. I think Paul loves me inside the way I do but it's harder. I don't know what made him say that though. Maybe from peer pressure? I'm kinda down!

10 MINUTES LATER

11/11/92 8:45 pm

Hi again, I'm crying now over Paul. I mean at least we're good friends and all but I loved him and nobody ever loved me. I wish someday somebody like Paul or my true love would say the same. I love Paul and damn I hope he loves me. This is a critical time in my life. Love is really getting to me. I need someone, someone like Paul.

I wiped a tear right here

11/13/92

Hi I don't wanna seem like every time I like someone and they say no I just move on. I still love Paul, but every time I look into Dana's eyes there's a click! I have to hang onto Paul. Dean said to have as many guy friends as possible because the ugly ones will be hunks soon. I wonder if Sean will be a hunk. I don't think so.

11/16/92

Paul and I were pretty close today. I'll always love him. Hopefully something cool will happen tomorrow ya' know. Something really neat. Maybe I'll get my report card approved by my dad for once!

11/18/92

Hi, today I found out that Paul and *Lisa* are going out. WOW.

11/21/92

I love Paul so much! I'm always thinking of him, I dress for him, I LIVE for him; I'm crazy for him. I hope he feels this way for me, ya' know! My heart pounds for him!

    I LOVE YOU PAUL!

11/30/92

I got Paul a hat, I gave it to him and he was all astonished about how cool it was and he was just like "thanks so much" Then he wanted to slap my hand for "cool." But then he hugged me in a really sweet way.

12/1/92

I love Paul so much! I don't know! I think we'll go out in the future. Wouldn't that be really weird if we get married? Let's find out.

12/2/92

I gave Paul a note and he asked me if I'm spreading a rumor that we're going out, I said no, because it's not true. I went to Science and told this girl Christina [about] it and she said he's spreading the rumor! God, not this crap again! FUCK!

12/3/92

Yesterday Heather Powers slapped Christina Orton for no reason.

12/9/92

Hey, today Paul and I goofed off in Technology, and we played *Street Fighter*. It was really funny. I mean it *seems* like we're going out.

12/10/92

Right now my life isn't really getting anywhere! Either is the relationship between Paul and I! In our hearts we're going out.

12/15/92

I got my school picture today, it looks ok I guess. Paul French kissed it! HAAHAHA. I'm not ready for a relationship. The song *Symphony of Destruction* is so evil! And I love it!

12/17/92

Today Paul and I were good friends. I know that we both wanted to go right at it right then and there. Well gotta go! I love Paul.

12/18/92

Today I found out that Paul likes this girl Megan. I guess I am JUST a friend to him. But I'm still in love with you, Paul.

1/5/93

Hey, Paul and I are drifting. And I kinda like John Dragonette! Ahhhhh. I haven't had my first *anything* yet. I feel so stupid, oh well.

Bye!

Rye

BLOCKHEAD
Vanessa Murdock

1991 marked the year I was no longer a little girl but a thirteen-year-old woman fueled by dreams and an undying passion. I thought as soon as my braces came off and my face cleared up, there was *no* holding me back from getting anything I wanted in life. I had a clear and *definite* plan, and a love for one man like no other.

Convinced that fifteen years later, I would be able to look back at my accomplishments feeling satisfied, I wrote this list of goals in my diary:

I hope I can read this in 10-15 and know that I achieved everything that I wrote!

1) Have the look and figure of a cover girl model for *Cosmopolitan.*

2) To be a hard working stage actress or singer/dance artist.

3) To be an opening act for the New Kids on the Block by the time I turned fourteen or fifteen.

4) Use my nice, sweet charming self to make Joe McIntyre fall madly in love with me. Not love at first sight, though, but a strong friendship that builds into an everlasting love.

Well, it's exactly fifteen years later, and even though the braces did their job and the tetracycline cleared my up acne (sort of),

Cosmo has yet to come a knockin'. No stardom, no Joe, NOTHING. I have failed at life and have the written proof to prove it.

January 2, 1991

Today is the day that I got you, you were a birthday present from my grandparents. Today is the second day of the new year and I hope by next year I will tell you that I have done everything I wanted to do, look way better in appearance, have the looks and figure of a cover girl model for *Cosmopolitan*.

I want to be in show business so bad it hurts. But not on the screen but the stage. My goal is to become a hard working stage actress and/or to be a famous singer/dance artist. Before I turn fourteen or fifteen I want to be an opening act for the New Kids on the Block.

I will be ten times better than any of the other opening acts. But when we go on tour I will be such a nice, sweet, charming, beautiful person Joe McIntyre will fall in love with me, not love at first sight but a strong friendship that will build up to an everlasting love. You probably guessed—I LOVE JOSEPH MULREY McINTYRE!!!

I know one day in about 10-15 years from now I'll be reading this. If so I want me to look in the mirror right now and look back on all my accomplishments over the past years. And I right now hope and pray to God that they will be what I said on these first few pages and hopefully many more pages in this diary.

Lots of Luv,

Vanessa

I Love Joe McIntyre with all my heart

January 3, 1991

I love Joe McIntyre! I love Joseph Murley McIntyre! I love J.M.M. I could scream this at the top of my lungs until I lose my voice. I love him so much my heart aches every time I see his face in a picture. I love what I see in the picture, I love what I read about him in books. One day in the near future I'm going to meet him and I know I'll love him even more in real life. Hopefully he'll love love me just as much. I know millions of girls feel the same way. But I don't believe we all express our love the same way so I think my love for Joe is unique.

Today me, my mom and my aunt went shopping at the Rideau in Ottawa. There was homeless people everywhere. I know that it is far worse where I live in Toronto but it still makes me so depressed. One of my other goals is to make sure everyone has a decent place to live and enough food to eat.

Love Always,

Vanessa

V.M. plus J.M

100% True Love

January 10, 1991

I love to babysit. Especially the Merrigans. Andrea loves Jordan Knight almost as much as I love Joe. But all of Andrea's dreams to be with Jordan are next to impossible because she is 10 years younger than him. I'm only five years younger than Joe so my dream isn't that impossible. My best friend Hayley and Melissa are so hard to trust with a secret. I know enough not to tell

them anything I don't want spread. That's why I'm lucky to
have you.

Love always,

Vanessa

I LOVE JOE MCINTYRE!!!!

January 15, 1991

Today is what people call dooms day. It's the day that Irac has to
pull out of Kuwait. In only a few short hours war might break
out. It's a very scary thought. I never thought it would ever
happen with all that was said about being a peaceful world. You
never know what this might lead to.

When—if—they send Canadian troops out to the Persian
Gulf my uncles will be sent out there. God only knows if this
will turn out to be World War 3. But I don't think so.

Love Always,

Vanessa

I Love Joe McIntyre more than ever!

January 16, 1991

Today I taped the New Kids "No More Games" video. While I
was watching it, dancing, having a good time I didn't realize that
the war in the Gulf had started that exact time I was watching
my beloved Joseph. I was watching the news and the anchors
were reporting about how missiles and bombs were dropped
every few minutes.

They made it seem like nothing too serious compared
to what past wars were like and George Bush made a speech
saying that everything will turn out OK—he hopes—but God

only knows where this war will lead to. It may end in a few days and it might turn out to be World War 3

Lots of Luv,

Vanessa

Words cannot describe my love for Joe McIntyre

January 23, 1991

I knew it! Today Jason Frame asked me out. I am so confused! Mellisa and Hayley think I should. But I really don't want to because I love Joe too much. I know I probably will never meet Joe. But I don't know what to do.

Love Always,

Vanessa

I LOVE JOE McINTYRE SO MUCH IT'S SCREWING UP MY LIFE (BUT I LIKE IT!!)

February 2, 1991

Today I went to the flea market. I bought three New Kids books and three New Kids posters. I am going to hang them up in my room tomorrow. I am so bored with my life. I want a total change. I want everything in life I can't have. But when I come of age I'm going to do whatever it takes to make me a happy person. I want to solve political problems. I'd do anything to get my kind of life. I am getting tireder by the minute. By the end of this week I'm going to be so tired it won't be funny.

I think Brian Benson kind of likes me. I kind of like him. But I love Joe McIntyre so much. If I knew him I would love him even more. That's why when the New Kids come back for a concert I will get the best seats and I will try so hard to go backstage. I have an idea for going on tour with the New Kids. I would be part of Special Request. I would sing and dance and the guys would dance and rap. I think that's a dope idea.

Luv Always,

Vanessa

If I filled my heart to the brim with love for Joe McIntyre it would be 10 times too little.

February 6, 1991

I have a long story of this weekend. The marina party was the most fun I had all summer. First I met Steve, one of the guys who Andrea liked, and his best friend. They were everything I stay away from. They smoke, they drank but there was something about them (especially Bill). Bill was the best friend. He was really good looking and had blond hair and hazel eyes.

Sometimes he'd just look at me and stare straight into my eyes. If it were anybody else I probably would have turned away but I just stared right back. He'd talk to me and Melissa and give us advice. He'd tell us how his life got screwed up and why. He told us what to look out for. He sounded like he knew us forever and cared about us.

When we talked alone I told him that Andrea liked Jeff and he kinda knew. He had got Jeff and Andrea together. And Melissa told him how I loved JoeMcIntyre and he understood.

He said he loved Madonna.

I think I'm in the middle of liking *and* loving him.

Love Always,

Vanessa

UNSENT LOVE LETTER

David Nadelberg

As a high school sophomore, I was determined to land a date with a girl I had a massive crush on.

The problem? I had never technically spoken to her. Rather than introduce myself, I devised myriad elaborate schemes to flag her attention. When those plans failed, I refocused all my energies and frustrations into a single letter.

But since she didn't know me, I felt compelled to use everything in my arsenal to "sell her" on the idea of just considering me. Thus, I desperately tried to be sweet but funny, serious but sensitive.

Truth is, when you try to be everything to someone, you end up with *no one*. I chickened out and never gave her the letter. What follows is one of many unfinished *drafts*, and the only one still in existence.

Hello Leslie!

How is your day today? Mine's quite well, I must admit. I do hope that yours is a good one, because what you are about to read may or may not add an extra color to the rainbow at day's end.

~~Listen up and put your mind at rest because for the few minutes . . .~~ First off, let me introduce myself . . . my name is Dave. ~~(Yep, that way cool guy who gave you this letter!)~~ For quite some time I've been, I've been trying to figure out a way to meet you. The older we all get and the more the time that we include into history passes on, it has seemingly become harder and harder to get to know one another. So, to keep up with the difficulties that modern times have given, I (have devised) 4 ways of introducing myself in the best possible manner:

1. I could've just called you, or simply approached and said "hi." But with that there's no enchantment or uniqueness. Besides, that means actually having to use (gasp!) <u>courage</u>! So I wimped. Sue me.
2. I could have also faxed you. My, wouldn't THAT be modern! Ah yes, but maybe just a bit <u>too</u> high-tech and impersonal. So then what??
3. Smoke signals?? That has so far only worked with Flies Like an Ostrich, a lonely Indian girl I used to know. Things between us didn't work out so well. She had this fetish for wearing large bones in her hair. She thought it was sexy and I thought it was part of her last boyfriend's left leg. Call me old fashioned but I still prefer those weird little scrunchy things. Anyway, smoke signals are definitely a "no-go."
4. So, what am I left with? Of course, write her a letter! Why not? After all, I've got nothing to lose but my dignity, pride, courage, confidence, self-respect, acceptance among others, sleep and honor. Sure, no problem.

By now you may be wondering just who IS this dork, <u>why</u> exactly is he writing me, how did he know my name, is he emotionally and/or mentally unstable, how long is this sentence going to be, and what is the most popular internationally played non-professional sport? Hmmm, interesting questions—especially that last one (to which the answer is rugby by the way). Actually, I'm a pretty good guy and I don't normally do this kind of thing. But I don't know . . . something here was just different, so I decided I MUST do this.

I'm so far glad that I have. Hope you are too.

To tell you something about myself, I'll tell you that I consider myself as an open-minded person and someone who wants to see things done fairly. People tell me I'm easy to get along with and funny. I love music, movies, sunsets across the water, beach volleyball, *Calvin & Hobbes*, the outdoors, classic lines and beautiful eyes. The last movie I saw? *Fried Green Tomatoes*. Favorite vacation spot . . . Utah. Teacher from ninja-hell . . . Mrs. Taft. Best pencil in the world . . . Choice #2. Most useless waste of a 30 minute time span . . . *ALF*. Pickup line most unlikely to work at school . . . "What time do you like to be woken up?"

ADULT ME SAYS

And oddly, this line was also crossed off.

Worst commercial tagline . . . "It's not your mother's tampon." So there you have it. The above is more or less what you might call a "Dave." I <u>even</u> have a romantic side. How about that! Basically, this whole thing has been a commercial—an advertisement. What sells to you might not sell to another. But, I sincerely hope you'll at least consider purchasing the product.

Here's a coupon!

Dave

ADULT ME SAYS

I drew tiny cartoon scissors gobbling up dashes like Pac-Man as they circled my name and number. It even said "Clip n Save!"

Addendum

Look, I hope you will consider this. I <u>promise</u> you that you won't be disappointed. Besides, how many times in your life do you think someone will give you something like this? I hope for you, *the answer is <u>many</u>*. But until then, all I ask of you is to just <u>try</u> me and see if you like me. From there on, your opinions are granted. Thank you.

I HATE DRAKE

Will Nolan

I was not a wuss growing up. I was, however, the kind of nerd that *other* nerds picked on.

I was a sensitive child who felt things deeply, but quietly. I was a free spirit, as long as I wasn't breaking any rules or hurting anyone's feelings. I was—okay, fine, I was a dork.

But I didn't deserve what happened to me. I didn't deserve humiliation. I didn't deserve Drake Renner.

The Diary of William Patrick Nolan, Jr.
April 10, 1982

11 years old

I hate Drake Renner. I hate him with every bone in my body. I hate him. He is the worse curse ever. I'm going to write it but I may throw it away because if my mom and dad find it I'll be sent away. I don't know where. They never say that part. But I'm so mad it's worth risking.

Drake Renner is a mother fucking ass shit hole. That's the worse curse ever and he is. I hate Drake Renner and I want him to burn in a really slow way that hurts a lot. Cause he sucks is why.

Today we were playing in a tree and he tied me to the tree and he took my shoes. He took my shoes! It makes me so mad my pencil is shaking. He took my shoes and threw them in the street. I couldn't get out of the tree and he went home. I finally got myself untied and fell in a puddle.

My shoes are okay.

But, so I told my Mom what happened. And she is in therapy and thinks she knows it all which she doesn't cause instead of being mad at Drake, she told me I should have said he made me angry. I said, What?! And I told her he was a fucker. I did. She was mad but I didn't have to sit in the no-fun chair.

She told me that I had to call Drake and tell him how I feel cause it's healthy and it's what she does with my Dad now but she does it in the garage so we don't see her express herself. She promised it would make me feel better.

I called Drake and I said, "Drake it's Will."

He said, "So."

I said, "I want you to know that you made me very angry today when you tied me to the tree and took my shoes."

He laughed for a long time and hung up the phone.

I told my Mom and she said it was time for dinner.

I'm never eating dinner again. Ever.

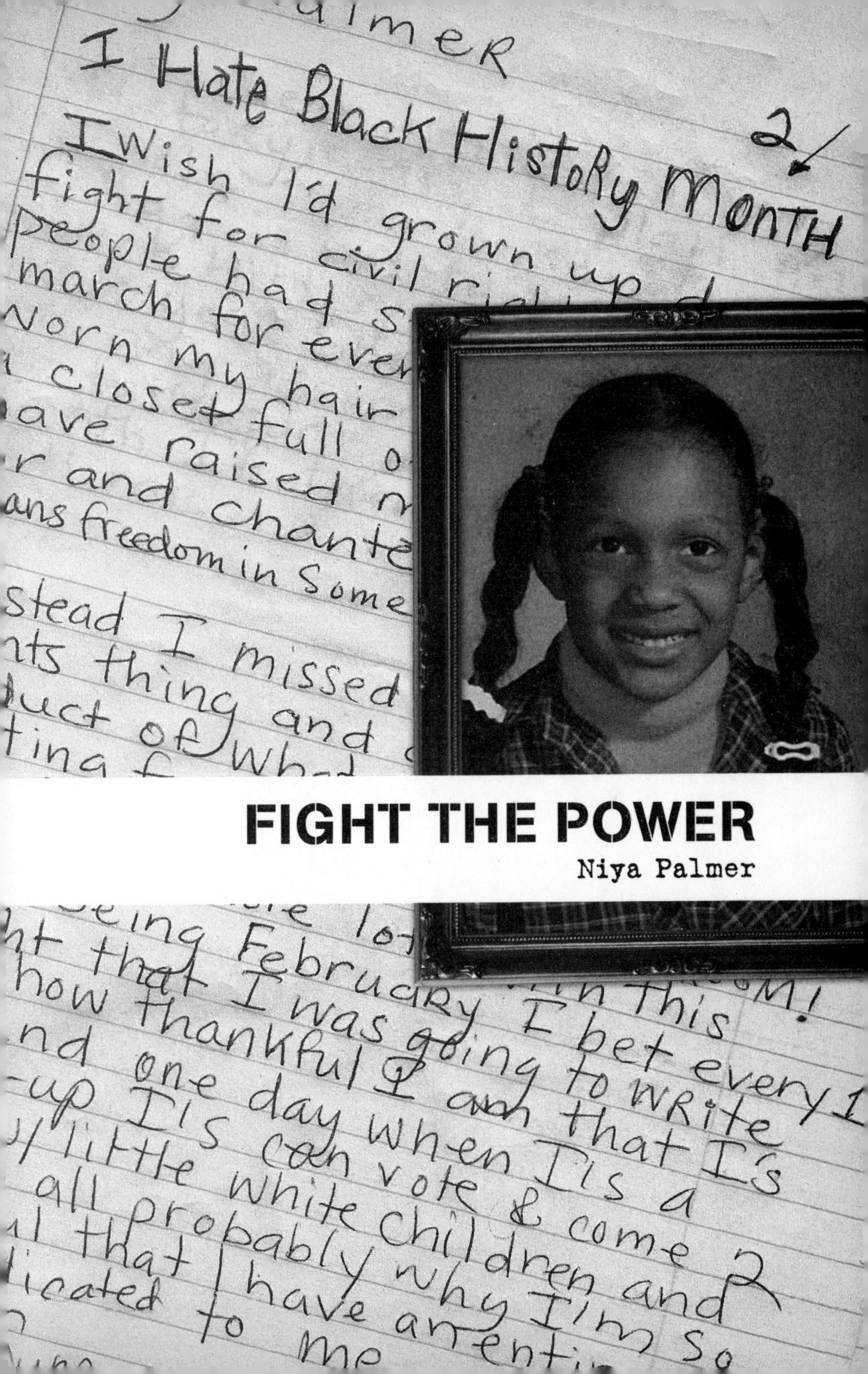
I Hate Black History MONTH

FIGHT THE POWER

Niya Palmer

When I was younger I fancied myself an *authority* on anything and everything. I had a vision that one day people would seek guidance from me, and, similar to a prophet, I'd be able to successfully guide them toward righteousness and truth.

With that idea firmly entrenched in my mind I took to writing my thoughts down so that one day I'd be able to have all of these ideas in one place, similar to a manual.

The following essay is a result of one of the most confusing times in my life.

Marriage is for Suckers

I'm never getting married; it's the biggest joke going. Marriage is the stupidest thing a woman can do to herself. At the prime of her life, she gives it all up to be a breeder for some sloppy man who can't even load the dishwasher or pack his own suitcase. Ask any newly engaged woman or newlywed what she looks forward to and she'll mention children. Just because you love children doesn't mean you should have them. I always compare these women to those poor misguided souls that became librarians because they loved books. I love peanut butter but you won't see me working in a supermarket.

I always thought that I wanted kids but I saw this special

on television and I changed my mind. The woman looked freakishly huge and she kept crying because it hurt so much and wasn't allowed to have a drink of water even though she'd been pushing for hours and was sweating and stuff. Every couple of minutes someone would come in the room and stick their hand in her vagina and then leave. For some reason she wanted to have a natural childbirth and do it without the drugs but halfway through the labor she changed her mind. I'll never forget the look on her face when they told her that she was too far along to get medication to minimize the pain. It was like last year when I went to Six Flags and my cousin asked me to get on a roller coaster with her and not to worry because it was very mild.

What I find *most* disturbing is that men are in the room. When did it become acceptable for men to witness their children's birth? It's completely unnecessary, labor is women's business. If by some unlucky stroke of fortune I do get married and get into a car accident, fall into a coma, become hospitalized, raped by an orderly and become pregnant—my husband will not be in the room. In fact *no one* will be in the room, not even the doctor. I would just be alone in a locked room all day until I had the baby. I'm serious.

Running is for Losers

My English teacher Mrs. Robbe, who also happens to be the girls' track coach suggested that if I run laps nearly as fast as I run my mouth, she'd love to have me on the team. I told her that while I was fast I wasn't stupid and wild horses couldn't force me to run around a track like an escaped slave.

Running is for losers; people who don't know what to do with their extra time. White girls who need self-inflicted pain to experience control and as a result join the cross-country team. It's for young women who secretly suffer from bulimia or anorexia and get to tell their story on every network created for and by women over and over and over again.

My grandma says that "some people don't have the sense to come in out of the rain," and I have to agree. What type of person runs fast and hard with no place to go? Dogs. That's the type of shit that dogs do. Dogs, and my next door neighbor Griffin who runs marathons religiously. He came to our house one day last year asking me to inform my parents that he was running a marathon and needed sponsors. Griffin is strange. He's managed to delude himself into believing that running helps him to think and clear his mind.

I told him when he began talking that mess that I get the same feeling when I'm drifting off to sleep and perhaps if he invested in a better mattress he could maintain a shred of dignity and not have to go around the neighborhood begging. He'd left abruptly saying he had errands to run, but I think it was the truth setting him free. Although, I'm not certain if the truth sets the person who told it free or the person who's hearing it.

This year when he came back to our door soliciting funds, I was able to share with him what my mom always tells me, that "God blesses the child that's got his own," and that he shouldn't ask anymore of our neighbors for money 'cause it's tacky. He should know all this because supposedly he's some big shot doctor. I feel sorry for his patients because I don't think he's wrapped too tight.

He left, but not before giving me the same look that Mrs. Richardson, my school guidance counselor gave me when she visited my class to discuss career goals with students. I told her that I wanted to be an OB/GYN and when she smiled and asked me if I liked babies I explained that I couldn't stand them but that I enjoyed "squishy things," and the idea of being in it up to my elbows was thrilling. This gurgle came out of her throat and she quickly got up and went to speak with my homeroom teacher who also became distressed. They left the room together and were gone for a very long time. Of course I could never be a doctor, I'm failing math. I'd only said that to divert her from my true intentions and I don't want her to laugh at me.

There's not much I'm good at, in fact there's nothing I'm good at and I'm going to the black circus when it comes to town in November and find out what I have to do to join. I have to be really hush-hush about it because I know how white people like to take stuff of ours over; everything but the burden and before I know it white girls would be trying out and in the end I'd be forced to watch a small army of over-achieving white girls prance around in unitards on a tightrope and that would just not be fair.

So, I thought I'd gotten my point across to Mrs. Robbe why I wouldn't be joining the team, until she showed me the uniforms. They're snap-away pants with buttons that run the length of the pant. They can be pulled right off, anywhere. Plus, they're green and that's like my favorite color so I went ahead and joined the team. Turns out I'm pretty fast.

I Hate Black History Month
In honor of Black History Month, February 11, 1995

I wish I'd grown up during the fight for civil rights. Before black people had stuff and we had to march for everything. I'd have worn my hair in an afro and had a closet full of dashikis. I'd have raised my fist high in the air and chanted "Uhuru" which I think means "Freedom" in some African language.

Instead I missed the whole civil rights thing and am now the by-product of what everybody was fighting for, the right to be the only black kid in the classroom. Thanks a whole fuckin' lot. With this month being February I bet everyone thought I was going to write about how thankful I am that I's free, and one day when I's a grown up I's can vote, and come to school with little white children and most of all probably why I'm so thankful that I have an entire month dedicated to me.

Surprise, surprise, I hate Black History Month. It's the one month out of the year when white people feel comfortable to ask me all sorts of strange, inappropriate questions and treat me as if I'm the spokesperson for the black race. How the hell would I know anything about black people? I can't even dance. Every year like clockwork when February rolls around I'm the mascot of equality. Thanks a lot Martin Luther King.

I hate the cardboard cut-outs of Ben Carson, George Washington Carver and Thurgood Marshall. I hate the laminated poster of Harriet Tubman leading the slaves to freedom. I hate projects that involve cutting out the shape of Martin Luther King's head and pasting it to a popsicle stick.

Last February in English class we had to sit around and

watch taped episodes of *I'll Fly Away*. Afterwards Mrs. Ellis lead a discussion as to why times were so much simpler then. Yeah, Ms. Ellis it was nice when blacks couldn't vote and the only thing we could hope for was an opportunity to clean up after your fat ass. Someone even brought in a copy of *Gone with the Wind*.

Two years ago we had an African-American celebration in the auditorium which still makes me cringe. It was an African dance troupe and they danced really hard, barefoot and pounded on a steel drum. Whose bright idea was it to present live culture to ignorant high-school students, at my expense?

I can imagine the committee meeting. "Let's have something authentic like; really, really black people basket weaving and beating drums." "I'd like to see brown children with big tummies . . ." "Oooh and flies, flies everywhere." That's authentic.

That was the same year that *Shaka Zulu* aired on television. I tend to divide my school years into two chapters; before *Shaka* aired on television and after. It was a 10-hour epic about "an illegitimate prince who reclaims his birthright with brilliance and brutality." Shit. The thing is the next day at school apparently everyone else had watched it. Instead of calling me by name I was referred to as "Spear Chucker."

This year I'm boycotting Black History Month.

I plan on getting a note from my parents. It will read: Niya is not to participate in Black History Month festivities this year. She's not allowed to partake in any assemblies, write any reports, or take part in discussions this month. If there's a problem please call us.

MARK INTERRUPTED

Mark Phinney

My whole life, I was someone who missed the big red waving flags. When a wake-up call went off in life, I was the guy who hit the snooze button.

So when my girlfriend, Karen, threatened to dump me at nineteen, I did what any self-respecting, wildly immature, attention-starved teenager does: I panicked and blurted out a suicide threat. Apparently, you just don't say that. It tends to not win a girl back. In fact, it tends to totally freak a girl out and have her take you to the ER, where they are legally required to send you to a mental hospital for a "seventy-two-hour hold."

Don't get me wrong. I was crazy. And I *knew* I was crazy. And I knew I drove *her* crazy. But I was far too lazy a person to actually follow through on my threat.

The reality was, I didn't quite know just *how* crazy. I thought I had a handle on all my neuroses. I thought I could cure them by just using this hospital as a place to "hang out" a few days. So I took it upon myself to write "self assurance journals" in order to solve everything. No one told me to do this. No one told me to title them this. Hell, I'm not even sure patients are allowed to have pens.

The point is, I thought I could cure myself, heal myself, solve my drama, win back the girl, become a famous artist, be the envy of all my friends—and all just by writing in a notebook for a few days. Simple, right? This is what I *actually thought* while sitting in a hospital gown.

Mclean Hospital Day 1

These halls are a welcome change. After the leather bound restraints and an 8 hr. stay at MGH last night . . . I arrived here at 5AM, slept, got interviewed 3 times and got blood taken. I'm still not sure *why* I'm here or what this place is all about. They say I'll be out early next week, maybe less. I'm "short term". 0-14 days.

I have privileges already. I mean, I'm not a lunatic. I'm merely depressed! It's kind of like the Boys Club. I basically have everything I need—food, toothpaste, comb, deodorant (luckily I had some on me, *as always*). I don't look at it as missing a weekend but more like . . . taking one off.

I just tried to call Karen. She's sleeping. *Good* . . . I'll either try back today or tonight or this weekend. She's working all weekend. She'll think I called to apologize and that I'm home, but when she finds out I'm here getting the help that I need on my own—the help that she wants me to get, that she told me to get, to get my problem taken care of—she'll be glad and feel for me and *miss me*. I'll explain it all to her. Hopefully she'll visit me! If not, we'll see each other when I get discharged. Then we'll be together again, once my problem is solved, for our anniversary.

She knows I'm not insane cause . . . I'm not. I'm just depressed! And angry! And that's what this place is for. I'll have time to think and work things out here . . . and write . . . and read . . .

Once I get out, I'll get back on top of things—get my glasses fixed, write, act, diet, Karen, everything.

Well, I have to get to a meeting. Later.

Self Assurance Journal # 1

Any thoughts that I have of Karen being or having a great time or not giving two shits about me, I should exterminate. *She knows I'm in here . . .* and is worried and is thinking about me. She wouldn't go off and not care about me being here. We're still in love with each other and she knows we're *still "one"* and she probably *wants to* call me. Also, me being in here will *always* play a part in our relationship. The fact that I was in this place for help . . . or whatever.

I'm in a mental and I'm still writing and reading and studying and researching. I'll probably go back to school in Jan. and hook up some more there. I'm writing scripts, stories, theatrical pieces etc . . . I'm struggling with life and Karen. *I've got to get my glasses back.* I could go to California! I'm an artist, a writer.

Today might suck in terms of nothing to do. I'll probably shower, make some calls (maybe a visitor, but *who?*), read, write, watch TV, maybe go out, hang out. I'm outta here tomorrow! . . . Or Tuesday. I'll be back.

Meanwhile today, Karen will either sleep all day and go to work tonight . . . OR she'll hang out today and go out tonight with Denise or Mike, whoever, but nothing extravagant or fun. She'll be thinking about ME and how I AM. She *wants* to talk to me. I *love* her and she loves me. I'd like to start a script today.

Self Assurance Journal #2

I know that Karen is still thinking about me. She cares for me, misses me and is concerned about me being in here *and* when I'm out of here. She has *not* written me off or forgotten

295

about me. I'm sure she's over the initial anger and hatred and is starting to *assess* the situation . . . and is finding that *she loves me* and still wants to *be* with me.

Like I said, she wants to call, but she feels that she can't right now (which is understandable). However, she will call in the coming week and she'll want to see me and we will be together again . . . in a *healthy* relationship. I know that she is thinking of me, missing me and is concerned about me and wants to call or see me . . . *and she will.* She has not forgotten me and still loves me and I love her.

Self Assurance Journal # 3

I know that Karen is now (or will be) thinking and/or feeling like . . . "Wow, I haven't talked to him in days. I wonder how he's doing in there . . . or if he's out? I *miss* him. I wanna talk to him . . . but . . .I can't. Not yet at least. I hope he knows that I care about him. I should have been more receptive. I hate everyone! I need him. I wanna call, but I can't. Not yet. I really *do* love him. I hope he's doing alright."

She'll hear a song or see something that will remind her of me or us and BANG! That will be it.

I was sitting in the music room today listening to the Sgt. Peppers and *A Day In the Life* came on. I was alone and it really hit me. *Everything.* Why I'm here on earth. What I have to do. Why The Beatles broke up! I felt *a lot.*

This is gonna make a *great* script.

Self Assurance Journal # 4

I know for a fact that I would never murder Karen (or anyone for that matter). I'm not a murderer! I'm a pacifist, a poet, a comedian! Yes, I do have anger in me, but it's self-destructive! I hit walls and throw things *and* I'm depressed. I just yell, then I cry. But I have never hit Karen or raised my hand to her (or anyone) and I never would. I'm just not violent. It's not in me.

I'm also getting help for my problem now. I have "control" in me, it just has to be . . . worked. I just get mood swings and anger due to depression, but I'm healing myself. No more shit for Karen. *I love her.* And the ADD (at least in me) doesn't trigger anger for me. It's just the focus aspect. I do get violent and want to cry from it. I'm not crazy and I won't snap.

Self Assurance Journal # 5

Karen does not think that anyone is more intelligent or cultural than I am. She knows that I put myself down alot but she knows that I am . . . brilliant and cultured. That I have read and learned and "feel" *the poets, the artists, the writers,* etc. . . . That I know film (*everything* in film!) and literature (all aspects!). That I know what I'm talking about.

I just have to look better.

She knows that even though I'm a comedian, I'm also a poet and a writer and a film *genius.*

I ask myself (as I'm sure others do) could I ever kill? Am I capable of murder? The answer (for me) . . . "NO!" I'm not violent. Yes, I have anger but it's . . . (1) Self-destructive type and (2) It's depression .

I'm a writer! A comedian! I'm not violent! I can't even fight! I'm not crazy, cause I wouldn't know if I was—I would just go! When I think of violence it's towards "my art"—fiction, film, prose, etc. I've hit my low and now I'm on the road to healing myself. But it's *not* a murderous problem. Not at all!

Self Assurance Journal # 6

Tonight I saw a film by Peter Weir—FEARLESS. It was intense and thought provoking. But the film pumped a lot into my system as far as overcoming *my* fear, facing fears and demons and . . . *changing*.

I realize now that I will not die from any of my fears (or) I'd be dead by now. I won't go off in a car. I mean, two accidents, one major and many close calls, and (I'm) not dead yet! I won't be jumped or shot etc . . . cause I am extremely cautious. No diseases.

I want to CHANGE. I am going to write and look good and feel good again. Clear up. Get rid of my mental drawbacks. Face my fears and tackle them. Like, driving, for instance!

I'm going to *be* driven and love life and live it to the fullest! I'm going to help others—especially kids!—and I'm even playing with the idea of becoming a counselor.

I am *not* going to die. I'm going to deal with my problem now and heal myself. If anything ever happened to (her), I would crumble . . . or if it was at somebody else's hands, they would be taken care of. (But) I love Karen. I'm going to make her and I happy. I'm going to do what I always wanted to do. And I will do it with *no fear*. The writing, the weight, Karen, friendships, art, life, mental state, etc.

I live what Max in the movie lived through—my own car accident. I can beat my fears and do what I want! Live my life the way I choose when I choose!

A drastic change in me is coming about!

I love Karen.

GEEK TRIUMPHANT

Retta

At seventeen, I was a high school senior. One might have characterized me as a geek, too. And I was a bit high-strung. I was in every club: French club, math team, student government, cheerleading, track . . . and I "managed" the wrestling team. In the yearbook, I was in every club picture, sitting in the same spot, wearing the same shirt.

School was very important to me as a means of getting into college. In fact, there is more mention of my calculus teacher in my journals than my family. So the most pressing things to me my senior year were:

1. Calculus
2. Cheerleading
3. Boys

In that order. And when I say boys, I was a slut . . . in my head. I was still a complete and total virgin. Oh, and as I said, I was high-strung, so there is zero stream of consciousness in these entries.

9/14/87
I have to start thinking of college. My class rank went from 16 to 14. I'm pretty excited, but I hope to do better. Jenny went from 15

to 10. She's very happy. Well, I'm off to do my Calc for Ms. Koss. *The Wonderful Calc of Koss. Because . . . because . . . because . . . because . . . because . . . because if I don't she'll kick my ass.* Later dude.

9/29/87

Ms. Koss. test was postponed till Monday and we have no review. English Vocab test tomorrow. Physics test tomorrow and it's going to be unbelievably impossible. Plus in French we have a quiz on the hardest tense in the whole language . . .the subjunctive! MY LIFE SUCKS!!!

10/02/87

I had to go to work. I told Mr. Carlson that I had to cheer on Sunday so I won't be able to work, and he had a spaz attack. He even called me into his office with Dave from Security. He asked me what college I wanted to go to. I told him Duke and he almost doubled over. I guess he's never seen an intelligent black person. You see something new everyday.

11/17/87

I thought the Physics and the English tests were easy. The Psychology test is going to be impossible.

11/18/87

Psych test was easy. There was no essay, so that took a lot off my back. We had a French breakfast in French class today, but the croissants were gross. I got a 20 out of 24 on my Physics test! I was so happy! I rented *Top Gun*, it was awesome! Tom Cruise is such a good kisser! He uses so much tongue action!

302

12/01/87

Yesterday was the last day in November and I skipped school. Can you believe it? I had Gloria forge Mom's name on my absentee note today, it was pretty good.

12/02/87

Ms. Koss wrote an awesome college recommendation for me. Oh, also today Dennis and I got somewhat close. We held hands and he apologized for almost breaking my knee. I actually cried, can you believe it?

12/10/87

Dennis touched my butt, and I keep getting chills thinking about it!

12/28/87

You won't believe it. Mom . . . read . . . my . . . journal. Now she's gonna hate me for a while. She thinks I'm some evil creature. She thinks I date guys. HUH?! I wish!

I made Tollhouse Cookies. They came out pretty decent.

1/3/88

Mom told Dad about my journal. All hell broke loose. I'm just not coping with my situation. I have no real life. I don't know why I continue with this stupid one I have.

I'm gonna go study!!

3/18/88

The best show is on! It's a mini series called *North and South*.

It's SO good and SO touching! When I first saw it, it made me laugh AND cry. It was truly a roller coaster of emotions.

It stars Patrick Swayze, who I find to be one of the most talented and hottest, I might add, actors on the TV and movie screen today. Gosh, it such a great show!!

4/8/88
I GOT INTO DUKE!

CAMP LETTERS

Sascha Rothchild

I had been going to sleepaway camp for years, and, among other activities, I'd learned how to horseback ride, play the piano, and water-ski. But the summer before eighth grade, I went to a new camp determined to learn a new skill: French kissing!

I was twelve years old that summer and still had never had a boyfriend or even kissed a boy. And I knew it was time for that to change.

My best friend, Julie, who was my constant confidant, was at another camp that summer. But I kept her updated on my boy progress and exploits by writing her explicit letters.

Letter # 1

Dear Julie,

It is Sunday. So much has happened in the past 2 days. This letter is going to be sooooo long. First of all, I liked Derrick and Jeff. Jeff started going out with a girl in my cabin so I didn't like him anymore.

So I started to like Rick, Derrick's best friend. I became really good friends with him.

I asked Vicky to ask Rick if he liked me. When Vicky asked him he said "I like her so much, but I wasn't going to say anything to her because I didn't think I had a chance." So he liked me and I liked him!

It took him one day to get the courage up to ask me out but he did around 4 o'clock. Tonight we had a talent show (I was not in it). I sat next to Rick holding hands. On our way to the grove (the boys' cabins) I sort of frenched him but everybody was around so not really.

At 9:30 it was time for the girls to walk to their cabins. Instead I went with Rick behind the boys' shower. I frenched him 4 times for about 7 minutes each. That's about a half an hour. It was soooo cool. I frenched him soooo much. It felt so good. While we were frenching I got to 3rd base without getting to 2nd. I had my jean shorts on though.

I can't believe I got to 1st and 3rd base!! Can you?? I don't want to sound perverted but it feels really cool.

Now let me tell you about Rick. He is almost 15!! He is 5-11 and about 150 pounds. He has got the best body. It is really built. He is really cute, too. Brown hair, blue eyes, no braces. By the way, I took my rubber bands off!! That is very important. You cannot french with rubber bands!

Rick knows I'm 12. He doesn't care. He thinks I am gorgeous. Isn't that cool? He is for Anarchy!! He is so cool. His ear is pierced 2 times.

By the way, Vicky isn't going out with anybody.

Love,

Sascha.

P.S. This letter is for your eyes only!!

Letter # 2

Dear Julie,

I am still going out with Rick. This is our 11th day! I french him at least 40 times a day. That is no big deal. I have gotten to second base about 6 times, under the bra. I have not gone to third base. I repeat, I have not gone to third base! Don't worry. I don't think I would go that far. I was just so excited that I kind of exaggerated a little in my last letter.

All Rick did was sort of put his hand there for one second with my jean shorts on. We were standing up, also. It was not 3rd base. Definitely not 3rd base!

I love Rick so much and he loves me.

Vicky still isn't going out with anyone.

I love this camp.

Love,

Sascha

Letter # 3

Dear Julie,

Today is the 15th. I have been going out with Rick for 15 days. Not any more.

There is this girl named Callie. She is very pretty and sexy and a slut. She is 12 and is not a virgin.

The past two days rumors have been going around the camp about Rick and Callie fooling around. I asked both of them if it was true, and they both denied it. Today at around noon I found out it was true.

So, in the middle of lunch I took a big glass of milk, went over to Rick's table and poured the milk on top of his head in front of the whole camp. Then I threw the glass in his face, said "Don't cry over spilt milk, asshole," and then walked away.

Rick was so embarrassed. Everybody was cheering for me. And everybody hates Callie now.

I am really glad I didn't go to 3rd with Rick.

I was crying so much after that. So was Rick. He came up to me, and gave me my silver bracelet he was wearing back to me, said he was sorry, and walked away. He loves me so much and he can't believe he made such a stupid mistake. I love him, too, but I could never go out with him again. Callie and him did a lot. I'm not sure how much, but he sucked her tits and fingered her.

Rick was going to stay for 1 session but because of me he told his parents he wanted to stay for 2, so they sent the money. Now he is stuck here. Callie is only staying for 1 session. Thank God! I hate the bitch, whore, slut, fucker, asshole, bitch again.

The thing with the milk was awesome, though.

I wish you were here to help me through this tough time. Vicky is cool but you are still my best friend.

Love,

Sascha

Letter # 4

Dear Julie,

Hi. So, I forgave Rick. I know he loves me and is really sorry and he promises never to talk to Callie again. So, you know how I was wondering if I should go to third? Well, I did!!

I went to 3rd two times. A few nights ago we had a co-ed

sleepover. That was where I did it. Rick stuck his finger all the way up there. It wasn't gross at all. He also kissed my tits.

ADULT ME SAYS

I'm not sure when I started using the word *tits* but its disgusting. I say boobies now.

So, I guess you could say I have gotten really far this summer.

I don't know whether I should give Rick a hand job? If I did, it would be the last week of camp. Guess what I'm listening to? "Jealous Fellows"! I haven't heard that song in soooo long.

Love,

Sascha

Letter # 5

Dear Julie,

A lot has happened since my last letter.

First of all, I gave Rick a hand job. We had been going out for thirty nine days not counting the 3 day breakup. It was fun.

Second of all, I got caught drinking. This CIT from first session came back to visit and brought Bartels and James Original Wine Coolers. I had like three sips.

Third of all, I got kicked out of camp. I guess the camp really doesn't like drinking. Whatever. I really don't feel like writing down the entire story, so I will tell you when I see you.

Rick was also kicked out. He didn't drink or anything but was so sad that I was leaving, he lied and said he drank also. Isn't that sooo romantic! We miss each other so much.

I really miss you too!

Love,

Sascha

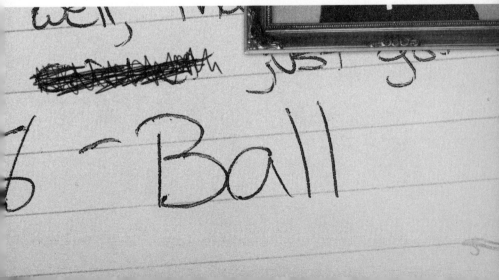

uth beach
night. I think I
eath wish. Anyway,
ught in
. Then I
n
d time.

MIAMI VICES
Sascha Rothchild

well,

just go

5 - Ball

I went to private school like most of the other rich Jewish kids growing up in Miami Beach, but I hated it. The kids were obnoxious and mean to me, and I was fed up with the snobbishness.

So for junior high, I decided I wanted to go to public school and experience a new life. When I was thirteen years old, I was thrilled to leave the uptight world of school uniforms, BMW car pools, and bar mitzvahs . . . and enter a world of sex, drugs, and crime.

A lot happened today. I made out five times with Jose Perez. He said I kissed like a rich girl. He had a long as fuck tongue.

I really like his best friend Carlos. I think Carlos likes me. Jose and I are just good friends but we fool around because we think each other is hot. I like all my new guys.

They aren't snobs. They're spicks.

They're more fun to hang with. I'm turning into a baser and I don't mind it. Nicole and I are friends again. Her boyfriend Leo is best friends with "my niggers" Carlos and Jose.

———

Today at school I saw the smallest man in the world. He was this girl's father's friend. When I saw him I thought he was a monkey. Then he started speaking Spanish and I thought, that's a smart fucking monkey.

I am reading *The Diary of Anne Frank*. It really means a lot to me. First of all, I'm Jewish and that means a lot to me and also I recently started writing in you. *The Diary of Anne Frank* has really inspired me.

Anyway, Friday after school Carlos and I finally made out. Nicole is being a real bitch. After I was with Carlos I spent some time with Tyrone, Trayon and Tyrel. I love them. I like black boys much more than white boys. They're more fun.

———

Hola. So much has happened. First of all, I'm basically going out with Jesus Rodriguez. I really like him. He's really sweet, funny, cool and hot as shit. And he has really good pot.

I went to a big party at Maria's house. The party was awesome. I got completely drunk and started talking to these older guys who had beer. They gave me a lot. Two older guys liked me and they wanted my phone number. One is 18 and one is 19 and they are both so fine. I gave them my number and told them I was 17.

I'm worried though. I'm turning into a bad girl. My grades are dropping, I'm drinking a lot, getting stoned, etc. I don't want to tell Diego and Shane I'm only 13 but I also don't want to get raped or anything. I don't know what to do.

I think I'm going to lose my virginity very soon. The scary thing is, is that I'm having so much fun. So many guys like me. I'm so fucking popular.

My mind and body are 17, but I'm only 13.

———

Hey. Wuz ↑ or ↓? Well, things are totally up with me. Mario and I are going out. I like him so much. He's so cool, nice,

316

funny, caring, sensitive and fucking fine. He has such a nice body. And he has a car.

Anyway, Diego, Shane, Mike, Josh, Rollando and Jesus like me but I'm Mario's. At the movies, Mario and I made out a lot and we went to second over the shirt. It wasn't a big deal at all. Then we smoked pot in the parking lot. It was awesome. Later Dude.

———

OK. A lot happened. First of all Mario and I broke up yesterday. I dumped him. The day after we started going out I went to his house and we were in bed naked together. Don't ask how that happened!

Anyway, we went to third and he tried to fuck me and he gave me a condom. I wouldn't sleep with him and I think he got mad. Since then it seemed all Mario wanted was to have sex with me. I broke up with him six days after we went out.

———

I think my Mom is losing trust in me, since she found beer under my bed. I can't believe how much I'm lying. And breaking the law. And cheating in school. What's happening to me???

Diego and Shane both called. I told them I was only 13, and they didn't even care! I feel so much better. At least I don't have to lie to them anymore.

———

Ay dios mio, well a lot of fucking shit has happened. I have been getting drunk and stoned everyday. Also, Diego and I broke up. I didn't mind that he was a drug dealer but it just wasn't working out anyway. Nicole and I aren't friends anymore. Squirrel and I are good friends and Sharron got a nose job. I haven't seen it yet. And last but not least, I'm going out with Antonio. We have been together for nine days. I really like him and I'm planning on sleeping with him.

Oh, and I tried cocaine! It's the coolest fucking thing on earth! I think I'm addicted. Oh well.

———

Antonio and I got a flat tire in the middle of Over Town last night when we were going to cop drugs. He was really mad and we got into our first big fight. What a temper. We made up though.

I like the way he makes me feel. I'm the woman and should be kept in my place. Of course, he is Cuban. Well, I gotta go change my tampon. At least I'm not pregnant yet.

———

Wuz ⬆ Yo?

I have done flake five times today.

I loved all five times!!!!! I'm not doing any more though. For now at least. I like it too much. The high is worth the low!!! I am also trying to stop smoking pot. I'm getting really burnt. Instead, I'm smoking cigarettes and shoplifting. I love it. I get such a head rush. Today I stole three pairs of underwear, 2 bras and 1 shirt. It was too easy!

Oh, and Antonio ate me out! It was too cool! I'm having an awesome time. I have never had so much fun in all my life.

Here's a poem I learned.

Cocaine, cocaine the sweetest fruit
The more you sniff the more you toot.
The more you toot the better you feel
So sniff a wiff and skip a meal!

———

Oh my God. I have changed my life around. I haven't done any coke in four days! I'm still smoking pot but no more cigs. School is good. I'm doing pretty well in all my classes. And I'm planning on fucking Antonio soon. He's the one. I know it.

Tomorrow Squirrel and I are going to the mall to shoplift from The Gap, Macy's, ect.

———

I think I have a death wish or something. Last night I walked around South Beach alone at 3:30 in the morning to cop some blow. And I got caught in a cross-fire. Scary! But I ended up at Denny's with Squirrel and had a really good time.

———

I did it. I slept with Antonio three times. It wasn't such a big deal. The first time it hurt a lot but the 2nd and 3rd it was much better. And Friday I had awesome sex on the beach. Not the drink! Haha. We did it at 4 in the morning on a lifeguard stand. I had my first orgasm, with a boy. It was sooo cool!

Also, this hot guy Damien is giving me a ride to school next week.

———

It has to stop. It all has to stop! I'm going to change my life around. I snorted two huge bumps and then came down hard. Real hard. The high isn't worth the low anymore. I have to stop hanging out with these people. I'm going to fuck up my life. I'm scared. Really scared.

———

Squirrel just scored an 8-ball!!!

———

Hi. I'm alive and not pregnant. I broke up with Antonio and I'm going to NA [meetings]. I've been off cocaine and pot for 20 days and I'm doing really well. It's really hard, though. I jones so much for coke, but I can deal. My life is good right now.

I'm still having fun without going crazy. I think I'm going to sleep with Jason. I really want to because he's so hot and he thinks I'm really hot. So many people do. I'm so popular and scandalous!

I'm leaving out so many details that I hope I don't forget but my hand would hurt if I wrote them all down. It's time for a new diary, but this one will always be most memorable.

Later dude.

GUIDO LOVE

Giulia Rozzi

At twelve years old, I had a torrid love affair with a boy named Jimmy . . . although he didn't know it. We dated for only one day, yet I was convinced that, in his heart, Jimmy always loved me just as much as I loved him.

The following diary entries chronicle six months of what became my three-year obsession with a teenage guido.

5/29/91

I love Jimmy, he is sooooo cute and funny. Everyone asked him if he would ever go out with me and he first said "Maybe" then "No" then "No." Today he called me a hairy bitch, but then said "Only joking" (I know he is joking).

I wish at the carnival he'd see me and buy me cotton candy and win me a big stuffed animal and we'd go on the ferris wheel and as "More Than Words" plays softly in the background we'd kiss. Oh God I love him sooooooo much!

I know you can't force a person to like you, but I think I am nice, pretty and funny. Everyone says he acts like he likes me but what is keeping us apart? That Greek God, I'd call him but his phone number is unlisted.

5/30/91

Today I went to the park with Dianne. Jimmy told me he went

to Jeanne's house and went to 2nd outside the shirt with her. He is such a horny toad! When I left, Dianne told Jimmy I would go to first and second with him. He was like "Oh really?" That's good right?

I really want to French Jimmy. He is so gorgeous. "More than Words" makes me want to cry. I'm crazy over Jimmy, it's all I talk about, it's so addictive!

6/24/91

On Wednesday June 19 I found out Jimmy likes me. He asked me out on a date for Saturday June 22 at John G's house with John and Lori. I said yes (of course). Seemed kinda funny that one day we are friends and then next day he likes me? We all went into the living room and sat on the couch. I sat with Jimmy's arm around me. He tried to French me but I laughed and bit his lip. Then Lori and john kissed so we did and it was gross and weird. His breath smelled like chicken and cheese. I was scared thinking I would screw up but if you kiss a boy don't you feel like a magic? I didn't.

Then I asked for his phone number and said "It's private, I'll call you." I knew something was wrong but I can't dump him. What if he really *does* like me? I cried that night cuz I was so confused. I should have been happy but I wasn't. The next day I got dumped! That SOB!

7/19/91

Let's see how can I say this without putting a downpour on everyone else, but life bites the big shit! Sure I am grateful, but I want it all. I can be so selfish, what about the hungry, the disabled, the prisoners of badness? Wait, I *am* lucky, but what do I want from this thing we call life? Jimmy. What am I stupid? He used me, (not like I didn't want to kiss him.) I wish he would come to my door with roses and take me for a long walk around the pond and sit by the water and then embrace in long loving kiss. But it will never happen.

Now just because I say I want to kiss him does not mean I am a horny perverted slut. Just because I wear eyeliner and makeup and my bangs up doesn't make me a slut. That's another thing, why is this world so focused on sex? I mean not to sound gross but sure sometimes I might want to see dirty movies and I want to experience it when I am older and ready. But boys are always like "Yeah I got some tit off that chick" or "ooh look at that girl!"

Guys can be so insensitive, why can't a guy be bold enough to cry? And another thing, every morning I look in the mirror to see if I look good and not to sound consited but I think I am pretty sometimes. There is so much pressure to impress people, When a girl walks by all slim and good-looking I hate to see boys drool over her like . . . hmmm . . . Jimmy!?

Looking in teen magazines, I wish I looked like those models. Well a lot of people say I am pretty . . . well I am pretty and I'll stay that way and if you don't accept me well too bad. I'm not about to change my clothes or hair or face for anyone.

I hate hatred and prejudice. I hate it when people lie to me. One of my friends claims she was raped, it is probably true but you can't be sure. I know I'm not an honest Abe and feel so bad for having lied to people before in my life and when I die I want to go to heaven so I hope God forgives and forgets because you are never alone because there is always someone in heaven watching us. Another thing I hate about this world (and this is only a small thing) why is the most popular insult "you slut or whore or ho or whatever you wanna say." I mean every person has given or received that word, and how would they know? I know I wear some eyeliner and makeup and wear my bangs up but that doesn't make me a slut.

My friend Kristen can take things too far. Like I tried smoking and she is acting like I killed someone and it's already something I feel bad about and then she thinks everyone at the park is bad but they're not and she doesn't like Jimmy after what he did, but that's quite flattering that she just cares about me (not like *that*, as good friends). Since we are talking about smoking, I tried it and I sorta want to again. I don't taste or feel anything but I like blowing the smoke out. But I won't or I could get addicted and ruin my reputation, have my family hate me, then get obsessed with nicotine and die . . . whew. God what am I thinking? I have a friend who did worse—he takes drugs sometimes. He was one of my friends but I think a lot less of him.

Well I can't list all the things I feel but let me say I wish life wouldn't be so hard, but without feeling pain you can never feel happiness. Live your life being yourself and see the world the way you see it. Always know where you stand you can dream and so be it.

Live life today and not in the past and don't live tomorrow till you live today 'cause if you jump the gun you'll throw your life away!

9/7/91

Wicked sorry I haven't written in so long! Right now I am listening to "Stairway to Heaven." It reminds me of dances when I danced with Mike D but never with Jimmy. So I am like "Okay Giulia let's like someone else" but today I looked into Jimmy's eyes and this is corny but I just can't like someone else when I really love Jimmy. I really want everyone—including Jimmy—to understand that I am crazy for him. He is my first TRUE love. Today he looked SO sweet in his Chicago Bulls shorts, UCLA t-shirt, and new cap.

I have "Every Rose Has It's Thorn" on, why am I listening to such depressing slow songs? The reason is . . . I know this is going to sound weird but I am *trying to cry*. Why you say? Well for some strange reason I feel like it and I heard crying is healthy. I am also pissed at school. I am not a geek, I am in the middle, but the kids at CMS are so snobby! They are nice to me and all but it's just that you have to worry about clothes, looks. TOO STRESSFULL! Then we work! Then (this is sick) but I am going to get my (.) soon. What if I am in school or talking to Jimmy!?!?! Can't we have an alarm or something? I hate being 12!

I know my b-day is in a month but still.

Today Jimmy asked me to hold his drink for him. Does he like me? This is totally a time for Dr. Ruth. It's almost 1 am, I just listened to "Heaven" and now I am listening to "More then Words." This outta be a tear jerker.

Maybe I love him cuz he is the first guy I kissed? No, that's not it. He's cute and funny but there is something more. I feel

327

like I know him too well. Like we are talking to each other *through our eyes*, ya know?

I wonder if you're thinking of me Jimmy? Jimmy? I hope you love me too. G-night. I love Jimmy. TL4eva!

10/26/91

Yesterday was my birthday and what a birthday it was. I cried for a half hour straight because of Jimmy. I saw *House Party 2* with Lori yesterday. It was cool. Then I called Jimmy and told him I really liked him. He said "Okay bye."

Right now "OPP" is on the radio, this is one of those songs I love and it would make me happy but I am too upset to be happy. I would be crying right now but I've been crying too much today and yesterday so I guess I am out of tears.

I have never been so in love with a boy and also so hurt by a boy. He always acted like he liked me, asked for my number, stared at me, it was so FUCKING obvious that he liked me, well at least I thought he did and so did my friends. Then yesterday (keep in mind yesterday was my b-day) I find out he likes Shannon. Today he was ignoring me and gave Shannon the cap from his Gatorade *and licked it*! I can't believe that! She had the nerve to ask me if I hate her!!!! Well, she said she might go out with him and that she does like him a little bit. She's such an ugly bitch! She can be nice but I am prettier!

Well, gotta go.

By the way, when I blew out my b-day candles my wish did not come true, right Jimmy?

THE UNHOLY LAND

Jami Rudofsky

330

At the age of fifteen, I went on a journey to Israel, the land of "milk and honey," to learn more about my roots as a Jewish woman and to discover who I am and how I relate to my religion.

What I ended up discovering was that I was very, very horny.

Day 1
Well at last the day has come to leave on a journey into the unknown. Emotions were running wild at the airport (especially with the mothers.) Anyway, we departed from Denver. After 27 hours of layovers, delays and searching endlessly for the pegs from a game, we finally arrived in the land of Milk and Honey.

Monday
Boy was today a BIG DAY! We got up early to go to the North. When we got there, there were hundreds of young beautiful soldier boys. I got my picture taken with the best-looking one. Then we proceeded around the corner to the statue of Hadrian (it had no head and I don't know why). Well, back onto the bus.

We headed to the Museum of Illegal Immigration before 1948. THANK GOD IT WAS CLOSED! We got a lecture about exodus and then we got to go to the beach of the Med. Sea. It was great and slowly but surely I was beginning not to worry about how I looked. I am also trying to just be friends with Lawrence because I know there won't be any more to the relationship.

I was in a good mood until we went to our next stop which was a small religious tour. I was so pissed at Barry because he was singing a song about how I couldn't get any from Lawrence. I can't even remember the significance of this town we were in where some schmuck was buried. Oh well.

Thinking the day was over they shoved us into a cemetery where Rachel was buried. The counselors all read poems while we slept. But one exciting thing happened. Lawrence asked me to be in one of his pictures.

Later we went to the Kibbutz. The food was surprisingly good, except I've got to stop eating bread!! After dinner I did some wash and I was also very horny so I went to Lawrence's room and he was sleeping on his stomach and his tush was right in my face! IT WAS BEAUTIFUL!

Well I was very horny last night and I could have gotten together with Evan because I guess he really likes me. So being the stupid person I am I went to his room and luckily I got in trouble for being out past curfew because I would have juiced it up with one of the stupidest Jews I know!! By the way, I got two letters today and I was psyched!

Wednesday
Today we had free time in Tel Aviv. Jody, Elise and I decided to shop. I found a really cute pink outfit! Some Israeli guy grabbed

me and told me he wanted to take a picture of me. HE WOULD NOT LET GO! Finally I hit him and he said "FUCK YOU" and I said "EAT ME"

Then we went to Jaffa and had some free time. It was kind of boring except at the end when I saw a really awesome looking guy. We had some smiling action. That was it for him. Oh well.

When we came back to base camp was a tragedy! All three of us were in our room and Evan came upstairs. I asked him if he would give me a backrub, which was a big mistake because first Suzi decided to leave the room and then Elise left. So there we were alone. So I deep hid my head in the pillow. I was so pissed at Elise and I was praying that Suzi would come back in the room. Thank god she did because he was starting to massage my boobs. Well then she did something that I later hit her for. She decided that she was tired so she told us she was going to turn out the lights. I told her not to because I wanted to write in my journal but she refused and turned out the lights and from there you can guess what happened.

I couldn't believe I actually let it happen. He is so dumb! And he is the shittiest kisser. In the middle of it all he asked if he should shut the door. I finally put my foot down and told him I was very tired so he gave me one last smooch and he left. WELLLLL, you can imagine! I ran through the whole building looking for that BITCH Elise (at the time). I couldn't find her so instead I came in the room and woke Suzi up and started hitting her. Then Elise came in and I totally threw her into the radiator. After that we all sat and analyzed the situation.

Friday

J.T. Day—Well today we headed to Tel Aviv to visit the Diaspora Museum. It was boring but then I couldn't believe it—I saw the beautiful guy from the night before! Unfortunately I never got a chance to talk to him.

Later

I went back to Goldstein Village and got ready for the concert. Finally at 8 we left for the big night! As we were walking into the concert area all of a sudden *he* was walking next to ME! I couldn't believe it! He said, "God, our itineraries are exactly the same because I have seen you before." I didn't know what to say because I was blown away! So then he asked us to come sit with him and we did for a few minutes but then we wanted to sit closer so we moved. After about 4 songs I saw him get up with his friend. He kind of yelled over to me, "Hey Jami!" It made me feel really good! By then I had to go to the bathroom really bad and some girls from their group said they were going to go pee so I went with them and they were really cool.

Well when we got back Elise approached and said, "Jami, he's been asking about you." I was totally psyched at that point! He came down to the concert area with Elise and I, and then Elise decided to leave and it was just him and me (oh, his name is Sean by the way.)

Sean and I went to the very back of the park. We talked about everything, LAX and the trip, etc.

Then something awesome happened. "You've Got a Friend" came on and I died! I turned to Sean and said "This is my fucking favorite song!" then he grabbed my hand and I followed

334

him. He took me to a place where nobody was and he turned to me and said "Do you want to dance?" I TOTALLY MELTED! It was the most romantic thing anyone has ever said to me. As Tamada would say, "I was totally creaming in my pants!"

After a little bit of close dancing, WE KISSED! It was an absolutely incredible kiss. After a few minutes we went to another spot where we could lay down. It was just what I wanted to happen! We kinda got really into it. God I literally fell in love . . . for one night! When we were walking back he said "God it sucks that you live in Denver" and I said "God it sucks that you are staying in Tel Aviv! Then he said "If I ever stop in Denver I will look up Jami." Oh God, he's great!

When I got back to where our group was, everyone swarmed around me. God I was in the best mood! I was so stoked that I told everybody about my romantic night!

Sunday (The last day in Israel)

At 5:15 we had to meet with Karen. About 15 of us stayed for such an intense discussion. I said that I felt changed. I know now that I will do everything in my power to come back as a counselor because I want to teach the kids like me all the things I have learned. Karen said what we have to do is help! That is the key word. I hope I can look back on this journal, years from now, when I am packing for my *next* trip to Israel!

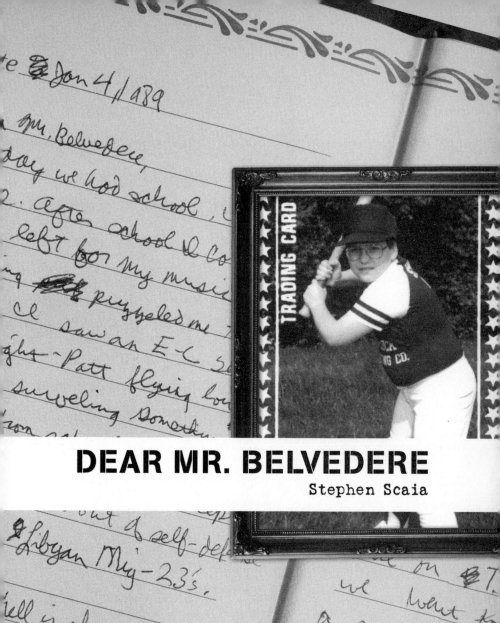
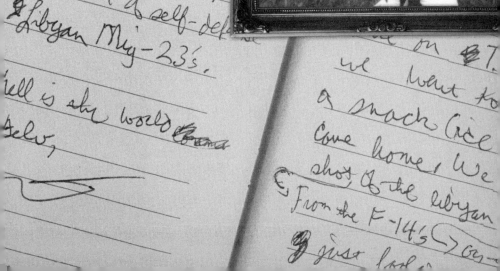

DEAR MR. BELVEDERE
Stephen Scaia

I was a fat kid. I had *no* friends and spent all my time watching television, hoping that one day I would find my calling, *any* calling (that didn't involve doing math). I got sucked in, thinking that in *one* of those shows about cops, doctors, or superheroes I would find something that would win me the validation of others and put me on the path to fortune and glory. Inspiration was harder to find on TV than I thought.

Then when I was twelve, our teacher gave us an assignment: Keep a journal. To help us, she suggested we write it in the form of a letter to a friend . . . but I was a fat kid and *had* no friends . . . so I wrote to my favorite TV star instead. Not Magnum, Remington Steele, or even MacGyver. I wrote to Bob Uecker's overweight, surly, vaguely gay butler: Mr. Belvedere.

The assignment lasted two weeks. . . . I wrote to Belv for two YEARS.

Feb. 22

Dear Mr. Belvedere,

Today we had school. It was OK. I got in trouble in school so I came home, napped, had a cinnamon roll for a snack, and watched *The Last Starfighter* (awesome!). I had French Onion

Soup for dinner (also awesome!) and watched *ALF* and *The Hogan Family*. They were all good.

It's awfully late now, Belv,

Steve

Rating: ★★★★3/4

Apr. 3

Dear Mr. Belvedere,

Today we had school. It was OK. After school I had basketball tryouts. . . . I didn't do so well. Then, I came home and had cereal for a snack and watched *Beverly Hills Cop* (Eddie Murphy was in it! But so was Judge Reinhold). Then, I had ravioli for dinner, watched TV and had a snack cake for dessert.

I'm starting to think I'm not good at anything, Belv,

Steve

Rating: ★★★★3/4

Apr. 5

Dear Mr. Belvedere,

Today we had school. It was OK. I finally realized how much everyone hates me. It made me kinda sick. But later, I made meatloaf for dinner!! Everyone liked it. Then, I watched TV for a while. We had blueberry pie for dessert!

Okay day, Belv.

Steve

Rating: ★★★★3/4

Apr. 9

Dear Mr. Belvedere,

Today we had school. It was OK. I got nominated (sort of) for Treasurer today. I don't know if I will win the nomination, though. It was kind of weird.

It's pretty late, Belv, but I can't sleep . . . too nervous.

Steve

Rating: ★★★★3/4

Apr. 12

Dear Mr. Belvedere,

Today we had school. It was OK. Ma took us to Taco Bell after. Later tonight I watched *ET*. MAN, it was GOOD! I hadn't seen it in like 6 years! So good! I'm going to bed now.

It rained, Belv,

Steve

Rating: ★★★★3/4

Apr. 13

Dear Mr. Belvedere,

Today NASA launched the first Space Shuttle Since the Challenger Disaster. It was OK. We got to see it in school. THEN, we had KENTUCKY FRIED CHICKEN FOR DINNER!!

I didn't get nominated to run for Treasurer afterall, Belv, you know?

Steve

Rating: ★★★★3/4

Apr. 14

Dear Mr. Belvedere,

Today we had school. It was OK. In school, the people with no demerits got to see "E.T." I know!! So, I got to go, even though I just watched it two nights ago! What a gyp! I just watched it!! After school I had basketball practice. It was really hard. We ran and ran and ran and ran.

I'm hurting, Belv.

Steve

Rating: ★★★★3/4

Dec. 20

Dear Mr. Belvedere,

Today we had school. During school our band gave a concert for the student body. It was OK. After school, I had to clean the bathroom. Then, I went to my band's Christmas Concert. We did excellent. After the concert, Ma stopped at Friendly's and let us get ice cream. I ate and ate and ate so much ice cream. It was great. Later, when we got home I watched some TV and went to bed.

It's the last day before Christmas Break so we've got a huge party in school tomorrow, Belv.

I. Can't. Wait.

Steve

Rating: ★★★★3/4

Dec. 22

Dear Mr. Belvedere,

Today I was too sick to go to school. I don't know why.

It was the last day before Christmas vacation, too. I was home all day and went to bed at 5:30.

So so sick, Belv,

Steve

Rating: ★★★★3/4

Jan. 12

Dear Mr. Belvedere,

Today we had school. It was OK. I got in trouble for something I didn't even do. When I got home I got in just as much trouble, even more. I watched a special one hr. "Head of the Class." It was filmed in Russia. It was about their trip to Russia. It was totally awesome. Ma bought ice cream and we had it for dessert.

Very educational day, Belv.

Steve

Rating: ★★★★3/4

Jan. 15

Dear Mr. Belvedere,

Today we had school. It was OK. After school Ma took me to Elder Beerman (a local department store) and bought me clothes to wear later tonight. Then, we went to Memorial Hall to see *The Pirates of Penzance*. It was GREAT!! Before the show we went to dinner. After the show I went looking for autographs and I got the star, Gary Sandy (you know, from *WKRP*) to autograph our programs. Then, we stopped at McDonalds and got sundaes! We got home around 11:45!

Such a great day, Belv!!

Steve

Rating: ★★★★3/4

Feb. 23

Dear Mr. Belvedere,

Today we had school. It was OK. I got tested today for the AP Class at the high school next year. It was pretty hard! Then, after, I came home and worked on my speech for the speech contest. Then, I got ready, and went to the contest, and . . .

I TOTALLY WON FIRST PLACE!!!!!!!!!!!!

It was great!!!!! After that, Ma stopped at Pizza Hut and got pizza to take home for dinner!! Oh. Man! What a great day!!

Huh, maybe this "writing thing" is where it's at for me, Belv,

Steve

Rating: ★★★★★

ADULT ME SAYS

Sure enough, thanks to Belv, I grew up and actually became a writer.

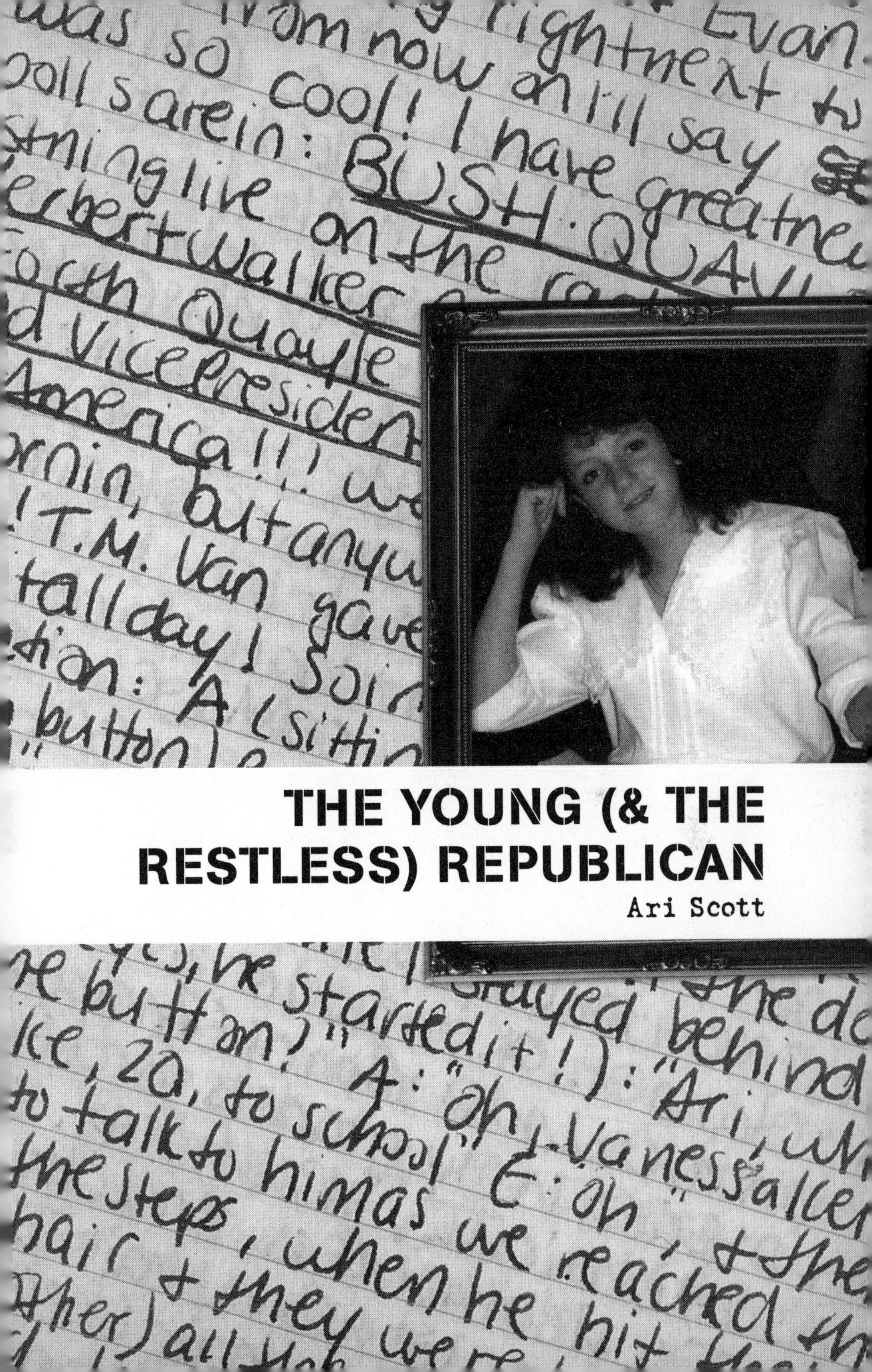
THE YOUNG (& THE
RESTLESS) REPUBLICAN
Ari Scott

The following are excerpts from my 1988 diary. There were two things I really cared about at age fourteen: the U.S. presidential election and a boy named Evan.

Luckily, Evan and I had something in common: We were both Republicans.

Unfortunately, politics was the only thing we ever really talked about. So while Bush/Quayle campaigned for votes, I campaigned for Evan's affection—poorly. I just did not know how to be flirtatious.

However, I did know how to keep a meticulous record of every single line of dialogue we ever exchanged. In the end, Bush/Quayle were more successful than I was.

Front Page of Diary
Personal Reminders:
Name: Ari Anna Scott
Address: Northport, NY

ADULT ME SAYS

This part I had added in.

Party: Republican/Conservative/Anti-Commie

I CAN TELL THAT YOU SNUCK IN HERE! LOOK AT YOURSELF, SNOOPING AROUND IN MY DIARY! AND YOU CALL YOURSELF AN AMERICAN, YOU SNEAKY VOMITOUS SLOB!

Tuesday, July 12, 1988
Dukakis has chosen Lloyd Bentsen, a Texas Sen to run for Vice Pres. I hope I soon find out who the next Vice Pres is. I'll know that when Bush chooses his running-mate (ha-ha!).

Sunday, July 17, 1988
I'm listening to a lady complain about how Jesse Jackson was not contacted about being overlooked for the Democratic Vice Presidency nomination. Oh, shut up. Vote for Bush and be happy with the outcome!

Thursday, July 21, 1988
Last night I stayed up late watching the Democratic National Convention and also did tonite. Mike Dukakis made his acceptance speech which I saw the last 40 min. of. Now it's over. In a month, the Republican National Convention starts. He didn't really say anything except about our country and jobs, etc.

Tuesday, August 16, 1988
Bush picked a running mate. His name is Dan Quayle from Indiana (Sen.). He's 41, good looking, and energetic. Beats Bentsen, anyway.

Thursday, August 18, 1988

Tonite was the very last nite of the Republican National Convention. Dan Quayle and George Bush both made their speeches—Quayle's lasting 21 min. and Bush's lasting about 45. Bush's speech was well-written, well-delivered, strong, hard, and one of the best speeches I've ever heard! . . .

Mom (voting for Duke) and I were talking (actually arguing) about politics. See, Quayle, while the Viet. War was going on, pulled a few strings to get into the National Guard, so he could avoid being drafted. Now it's turning into a big thing. And he's not bad-looking. They showed a pic. of him at age 20 or so and he looked a bit like Tony O'Dell ("Head of the Class").

Friday, September 16, 1988

I bet Jess, Vanessa, and Bonni each 2 brownies that Bush will win. I actually bet Jess 2 Almond Joys, but only if I lose. Yum yum!

Wednesday, October 5, 1988

I saw the Vice Presidential debate—it was a bit boring. Poor Dan. Mom made fun of him the whole time. The debate was pretty even.

Tuesday, November 8, 1988

Today was so cool! I have great news—the polls are in: BUSH-QUAYLE!!! I'm listening live on the radio to Bush! George Herbert Walker Bush and James Danforth Quayle are the new President and Vice President of the United States of America!!! Well, not until they are sworn in, but anyway, I talked to Evan today! This morning Vanessa gave me a Bush button and I wore it all day! So, in math, here's the conversation:

> Me (sitting at desk): "Evan." (hold up Bush button) "Bush!"
> Evan (smiling): "Yeah, Bush!"

Also, on the way out the door of math . . .

> Evan (yes, he started it): "Ari, where'd you get that button?"
> Me: "Oh, Vanessa brought like, 20 to school."
> Evan: "Oh."

And then I planned to talk to him as we reached the bottom of the steps, when he hit the back of Jessica's hair and they were talking all the way to English. I swear to God, I'm walking with him tomorrow! I will! I'm gonna talk to everyone! Greg S. and Peter R. and a lot of people are for Bush!

Wednesday, November 9, 1988
First of all, Bush is not the actual President until January 20. Boy, what a great day!

I am so glad Evan is for Bush! Here are our conversations:

In Math, he said "Bush" and we smiled at each other.

At our desks I turned around and me and him and Jennifer and a couple other people were talking and I said to him something like, "I went with my mom to vote," or whatever.

In English, Evan and Scott were talking about Bush and Dukakis and I was watching them and Evan looked at me and said "Bush!" and I made a fist and said "Yeah" or "Bush." Then

I asked Scott if he was a Democrat (he was) and Evan sorta pointed at me to tell Scott I was talking to him. The biggie came while we were walking out of the band storage room.

Me (holding up Bush bumper sticker): "Evan."

Evan: "Bush! Where'd you get that?"

Me: "Oh, at the social studies resource room. I got like, 2 of these and a few stickers. So, I went with my mom to vote—she voted for Dukakis."

Evan: "Ohhh!"

Me: "I know. I was thinking like, what would happen if I accidentally stuck my hand in [the voting booth] and it slipped and hit the wrong thing. 'Cause I was sticking my head in . . ."

Evan: "You were in the voting booth with your mom?"

Me: "I was just sticking my head in, but yeah, my whole family was in there—all my sisters."

Evan: "That's illegal, you know."

Me: "It is? Are you sure?"

Evan: "Yeah, it's illegal."

Me (shrugged): "Oh well . . . bye."

Evan then went to his locker while I talked to Vanessa and then I went to my locker. While I was walking outside to find my bus, I passed Evan. He's like, "Bush Bush Bush Bush!" I smiled and made a fist and said "Bush!" and before he said anything I just lifted up my hand, waved, and smiled.

Monday, November 14, 1988 (in math)

Me: "Evan—I found out that Bush and Quayle are related! They're 10th cousins!"

Evan (raising eyebrows): "Really?"

Jennifer: "Wait, Ari, where'd you hear that?"

Me: "On the radio this morning." (she looks skeptical) "I swear!" (and to Evan) "They're also related to Abraham Lincoln!"

Evan: "Are they allowed to do that?"

Me: "I don't know."

Then Jennifer said something. But that was it . . . isn't that crazy? It's true—Bush and Quayle are 10th cousins! Not only is Bush related to the Queen of England (I already knew that) but they are also related to Abraham Lincoln, Marilyn Monroe (which I forgot to tell him) or actually the father of Marilyn Monroe.

Everyone I tell that who was for Dukakis is like, 'oh, that's nice.' I just think it's fascinating.

Nobody in my family does, though.

ADULT ME SAYS

I soon found out that Evan had a girlfriend. We remained acquaintances for a while before eventually drifting apart when we got to high school.

A few years later, I was in my first serious relationship and began to wonder about what I would do if I got pregnant. I rethought my stance on being pro-life and decided I no longer wanted to be a Republican.

COURTING CATHOLIC GUILT

Victoria Scroggins

In March 1997, I wrote this journal entry. It was my senior year, I was eighteen, and I had fallen head-over-heels, crazy, madly in love. I was one of the few—okay, maybe the *only*—girls at my all-girls Catholic boarding school who had a shaved head and carried the sweet vibe of youthful lesbianism with her.

I was coming to terms with my own sexuality, as young, all-girls boarding-school students are prone to do. Fortunately, I didn't encounter a lot of resistance to my budding homoness. I was just spending my days hanging out with friends, sneaking cigarettes and beers, and dating girls from other religious schools in the area.

All of that changed when the most amazingly beautiful girl walked into my life and my art history class. I'm not entirely sure what thoughts crossed my mind when I first saw her. The unbearable clenching and knotting in my stomach and the deafening heartbeat that rang in my ears were too distracting. All I know is that from that moment on, I was hers, if she would have me.

Given the fact that my concept of love was gleaned entirely from movies, I didn't expect that giving my love and getting it back would be as troublesome a thing as it proved to be. I mean, Lloyd Dobbler got the girl, and I didn't even get a pen.

All I wanted was to see that love come to fruition. Unfortunately that proved to be a little more difficult than I had imagined—well, a lot more difficult, actually.

Dear Diary,

So I know I haven't written in a while but I thought things were going really good. It seems I only write when things are going shitty.

I just got off the phone with Caroline. God damn it. God damn it. This is bullshit. Caroline tried to be nice about it but what can you do with that kind of information. I mean there's no real way to soften that blow. Oh well. Thanks for trying Caroline. I have no fucking idea what to do. I mean what the fuck????

I can't believe Katherine is so fucking stupid. Or that religious. I didn't think she was that religious but I guess I was once again wrong. I mean that's fucking bullshit. The thing is, what do I do now?? Do I call her?

Caroline said that Katherine didn't want me to know. Well, no shit. It's embarrassing to let people know that you're crazy. I don't know what to do. I mean she's leaving for spring break in two days and then I won't see her for a week. Maybe that's the best thing. Maybe if I just let her go, things will be ok. I can go to Masami's party and have a kick ass spring break. Katherine can just sit on her ass on a fucking beach somewhere and make out with some local skeeze. Fucking nightmare.

But what if she wants to talk to me?? I mean, I want to talk to her. What do I do? If I call her and she doesn't want to talk to me, then what?

Do I just take that rejection? That double rejection? Do we just stop talking and that's it. We kiss and then that's it? She's gone back and forth for so long. No way. Fuck her. I just don't think I can take it anymore.

She wants to question, then let her do it on her own. But, I am crazy about her. I don't want to stop talking to her. I know I couldn't stop thinking about her. Katherine. Me. What do I do?

All I know is that when she held my hand and we finally kissed last Thursday, I thought everything around me, including my body was going to burst into flames. I mean, I am crazy about her. Crazy.

Why did she have to throw up?? Why?

Is this a test?

Some sort of shitty test about how much crap I can take?

I've liked her for so long and now she likes me and then she has to vomit right after kissing me? And she has to think that it's God's way of punishing her? This is what is fucking happening? Oh my God. Holy shit. This fucking sucks. All girls schools suck. Well not totally but this girl sure fucks up the whole picture.

Should I call her? I'm going to call her.

I'll be calm, cool, and inquisitive. That's it. I'll just take this fucking bull by the horns and get gored. Hemmingway would grab the bull. But he was also Hemmingway. Oh man. It can't get worse right. I mean she's already thrown up after kissing me, it really can't get any worse.

I'm going to call her.

Ok, later paper.

THE GUIDING LIZA
OR, A FAMILY FRIEND-OF-DOROTHY
William Seymour

This is from the first of many journals that I started writing when I was fifteen. My parents had just divorced, so I had to give up my two dogs and four hamsters and move to a new city with my mom.

I had no friends. I didn't know anyone. I was the "new guy" at this strange high school. And there began my definition of hell.

I got beat up and harassed regularly, so I either cut classes or ditched the entire day. The only way to get away from my problems was to write and get wrapped up in *other* people's drama (i.e., a hefty addiction to a certain soap opera). I shoplifted and struggled with my sexuality.

Just when it couldn't get worse, something *amazing* happened: My mom got a job working for the greatest gay icon known to man. It changed my life forever.

September 20 (1980)
We left San Diego this morning to move to Lake Tahoe. No big news, just sad news.

September 22
Today was my first day of school. I was so scared. Everyone knows I'm the new guy, and I'm totally behind too. I think I hate it here.

October 1

Today a sophomore named David said he was going to "kick my ass" after school. I don't even know him! I don't know anybody! I'm so bored and depressed. I got home early today and watched this soap opera called *The Guiding Light*. It was <u>really good</u>.

October 9

UPDATE: Mom got a job! She's working with the actress lady Liza Minnelli. She needs Mom to be her assistant while she's pregnant. Neat-o huh?

I'm very behind in French. No big.

October 10

I ditched P.E. class today because I didn't want to play baseball and get made fun of again. After school I went to Mom's work and met Liza Minnelli and had a good time, and then later I met Bill Cosby.

October 14

I <u>had</u> to ditch school to watch *The Guiding Light* again today. I just love to see it. They almost seem like friends to me. I knew today was going to be a <u>shocking</u> episode! Mrs. Wexler died today! She was sort of a wicked woman, but I still feel very sorry for her. I can't <u>believe</u> she's dead!

October 15

There's this guy named Jason (I think) and he's really been making fun of me and embarrassing me so I ditched my P.E. class today. I was afraid to see him and all my enemies. When

I got off the bus after school today he said "I'm sorry." I was totally shocked!

October 22
Today a whole group of kids were going to beat me up after school but thank God they didn't. Maybe they forgot. Some people just <u>hate</u> my guts! Liza Minnelli sang a song for my Mom at work today. I'm very jealous. I don't know why.

    UPDATE: I have a new hobby idea. Mapping!

October 28
I went back to P.E. class today; they've started a soccer unit. I had to ignore all the mean comments . . .

1. I'm not going back until they're done with soccer.
2. My Mythology study group is doing a presentation in front of the class on Friday, so I'm going to miss that day for sure too.
3. I have <u>a lot</u> of days I need to miss.

November 4
Election night. Well it looks like Ronald Regan is the President. Today I told Liza Minnelli that I don't like school. She said she went to lots of different high schools and she didn't like school much either. (I think I like her.) Even though I only go to school a few days a week, I've gotten great grades, except in French.

November 6
Today I must have cried all afternoon, just because of it all. I ditched typing today which is my last class. I'm so bored. I've

started work on writing my own soap opera; it's called *Love of Nerd*.

November 21

I stayed up tonight and found out who shot JR. on *Dallas* then I went to bed at 3 a.m. because I was writing.

December 1

Snow! I wore my new "moon boots" today and I ditched P.E. because I heard they started a basketball unit. I think I'll stay away until they're done with that.

December 2

I ditched school today and I went to Safeway and <u>I saw my Mom in the store</u>! Luckily, she didn't see me. I stole an $8.00 necklace and a $2.00 scarf. I don't know why.

December 7

I haven't been to P.E. class in six days 'cause of ditching the class or just cutting the whole day. We didn't go to church today because the car wouldn't start. Mom is very upset, she said for us kids to just go live with our Dad. I watched *Hero at Large* and then *The Muppet Movie* on HBO, and then I made some lemon bars.

December 8

Today I cut P.E. and my French class—I had to read a speech out loud and I didn't want to. I took two books from Raley's Grocery Store today. I don't know why.

December 10

I was sick today, for real life, so I didn't go to school. I went to the store with Mom, and while she was getting things, I stole two *Cracked* magazines. *The Guiding Light* was real fine today. I just loved it, it's so mysterious. There are so many secrets!

UPDATE: I'm making potholders for a new hobby.

December 12

Didn't have to go to school today! I got up very early and went to Liza Minnelli's house for a taping. I mean, "Aunt Liza". That's what we're going to call her now. Mom wanted us to call her and her husband Mr. and Mrs. Gero, she says it's more respectful. Liza didn't like that, so now it's Aunt Liza and Uncle Mark and it's all figured out.

When NBC's *Today Show* got there they set up her living room to do a spot on the show where she's reading *The Night Before Christmas* to a bunch of little kids. My sister got to be one of the kids listening to the story. I met the director, the camera men, the monitor people, the make-up girls, the set designers, and all the others too! I worked on the set and decorated the tree and made décor with the designer and then fanned the tree during the taping so the tinsel sparkled.

After all the taping, they cleaned up and the director said I could have all the left over glitter, spray paint and ribbon! Then, Aunt Liza said she wanted her family to have a picture, so my sister sat on her lap and I sat by her side and my mom took a picture.

December 13

I went to Aunt Liza's house today. We were watching TV in her room and she asked me to answer the door, when I did, it was that guy Sammy Davis Jr.! I didn't know what to do! We all sat down in the living room and talked about Aunt Liza and stuff and then we compared soap operas. He liked *General Hospital* and I told him, of course, all about *The Guiding Light*. He said he might check it out! Then he shook my hand and left. Later, Aunt Liza and I watched the show and she said she liked it. Amanda was her favorite too. (Now, I *know* I like her).

UPDATE: <u>Aunt Liza has a hobby too</u>! Needlepoint! She's sewing a green turtle on a little pillow.

December 14

The NBC truck came to our house today! Aunt Liza had the Christmas tree from the taping at her house delivered to <u>our house</u> so we would have a tree! We got to decorate it and everything. It was so huge it got all the way up to the ceiling.

December 15

I need to go back to school sometime next week so today I cut school and stole some bandages, straps and chocolates for an excuse from P.E. class. I don't know why I stole the chocolates.

December 16

Today I cut school again. I'm not ready to go back. Jennifer Richards was found guilty of the second degree for murdering Mrs. Wexler! I can't believe it! She was in total shock in the courtroom. They all think she committed the murder! I know for a fact she's innocent! I think I'm addicted to *The Guiding Light*.

UPDATE: Oh My God! A note came in the mail about my grades (a 'D' in French) and someone from school left a note for my Mom and wants to know about my attendance! I'm definitely going back to school tomorrow.

December 17
Today was my first day back to school in awhile. I wore all my bandages and I wrote a note that said I had torn ligaments in my knee. The P.E. teacher said I needed a note from a doctor. SO, after school I stole some nice stationery paper and typed a rough draft from "a doctor."

UPDATE: I have a new hobby! I'm making wreaths out of salt dough.

December 18
Today the note I typed was cleared by my P.E. teacher Mr. Orlick and now I don't have to participate in class. I never want to go to P.E., ever.

December 20
Tonight I went Christmas caroling. We went to John Davidson's (he's staying next door to Aunt Liza in Paul Lynde's house) after that we went to Aunt Liza's and then we went to Caesar's Tahoe to see a show (it was just okay, not great). When I got home, I wrote a Christmas play for church, and made two more wreaths out of salt dough.

December 22
Journal, this is serious. After I went skiing this morning, I was

playing with my sisters, and Mom came home from work and told me Aunt Liza might lose her baby. She's very sick and she's in the hospital. They are working really hard so she won't lose the baby.

December 23

Aunt Liza and Uncle Mark won't be here for Christmas. I'm so sad. I really love Aunt Liza. I went to her house today and I found her address book. I went to the 'S' page and I put my name, address and telephone number right under Neil Sedaka's . . . just in case she ever needed to write me or call me.

December 24

Christmas Eve. Aunt Liza lost her baby. Everyone is really sad. I'm <u>so sad</u> about <u>everything</u>. We only have one present each and Mom says we have no money.

I went to the grocery store and stole three books and two magazines. I don't know why.

The Christmas play I wrote for church went just fine tonight.

December 25

Christmas Day. We went to Aunt Liza's and had a Christmas brunch. Uncle Mark's family was there but Aunt Liza was still in the hospital with Uncle Mark. Their Christmas tree was really pretty. It was cute and small, with little glass ornaments from each character in the movie *The Wizard of Oz*. All three of us kids got <u>tons</u> of great presents! Aunt Liza gave me books about her mom (the girl from *The Wizard of Oz*). And Uncle Mark's family gave me a record by the singer Bruce Springsteen and a really cool wood puzzle-game from Italy.

January 4, 1981

Aunt Liza said she would autograph the books that she gave me for Christmas as soon as she could. I really don't want to go to school tomorrow. I hate all the kids there.

January 20

Today the Iranians finally let out the hostages! There are so many wicked people in the world. Anyway, *The Guiding Light* was a really good today. Amanda and Morgan are friends again! I took a picture of the TV at the end of the show so I could always remember it.

January 22

I got through my finals okay. It was a half-day so I saw My Show just in time! Everything is out in the open about Jennifer. Tons of secrets O-U-T, out! Thank God! But, Amanda lost her baby and she might die, just like what happened to Aunt Liza. I went to "Home Ministry" at church tonight and I gave the $1.25 that I stole from my Mom.

February 9

I discovered a big lump under my chin today.

February 16

No school. It's Washington's Birthday! I can't believe my vacation is completely gone!! I'm afraid of school. During the week off I was supposed to do a book report and also a term paper. Neither is done. I haven't even begun the book report OR even read the book! My lump really hurts too.

February 18

I saw my school counselor about the lump on my chin and my problems at school and she advised me to go to the Eldorado Health Department. I asked her about my P.E. class—not too much happened on that. I miss Aunt Liza.

February 19

I went to the Free Clinic and saw Dr. Weidman. She said I have a big cyst that is basically a bacterial problem. She cleaned it up and then she gave me some penicillin. Now I have to wash my lump with a medicated soap. It's so gross.

February 20

Mom agreed to talk to my school counselor Mrs. Stuck about getting out of P.E. class permanently. I guess things on *The Guiding Light* are okay but I'm really busy right now.

March 2

Mom met with Mrs. Stuck today. I'm temporarily going to be a library aide instead going to P.E. class but I had to agree to go to counseling at T.R.Y.S. (Tahoe Runaway Youth Services) even though I'm not a runaway. I'm fine with that. I don't care. I haven't seen *The Guiding Light* in SO long. I hope everyone is okay. Tonight I watched *Eight Is Enough* and then the *Love Boat* and went to bed.

I stole a bottle of malt flavoring at the store today. I don't know why.

March 27

I finally got to see *The Guiding Light* today. It was pretty good.

It just seems like <u>a lot</u> of the same things are going on, and on, <u>and on</u>.

April 6

Today is my 16th birthday. I had the worst day ever. Nobody really knows me except all the people who call me fag and stuff. Tonight, Mom is taking me to the Barry Manilow concert.

April 20

No school today! I got to see *The Guiding Light* it was really good, and then my sisters and I went to the lake and did a "blind experiment." I blindfolded myself for two hours and I walked around. I think I should write down my experiences with that.

April 28

JOURNAL, YOU WON'T BELIEVE THIS! Today, I cut school and went to the grocery store. I stole a Liza tape and a Mountain Dew, and then I took the bus to Payless. When I got into Payless I picked up a bottle of Vivarin next to the NoDoz. I put it in my pocket and walked around for awhile. Then, I went through the turnstile to leave and two security women asked me about stealing! They took me to the back office and then questioned me at a table and sorta booked me or something. My counselor Chuck from T.R.Y.S. had to come and get me and then I had to talk to him for a really long time.

So far nobody is going to tell Mom.

May 4

We started this unit in school where we have to take care of an egg like it's our baby. Mine is a girl and she's real good-lookin', I named her Peggy.

May 5
SCARIEST UPDATE EVER: There was a letter in the mail from Payless Drugs. They want me to pay a $100 fine for shoplifting! I almost died!! I don't know what to do! I really miss my dog, I hope he's okay.

When I got home I killed my egg Peggy and I made another one. Now, it's a boy named Eggbert!

May 13
Today I cut school and called Payless to see why they want $100, and the Payless man said that it was the minimum charge for damages!

May 20
I cut school again today. I had so much to do. I met with Chuck, he called a ton of people and by Monday he might have a way for me to work at the store to pay off the fine. Then, I applied for a Social Security card so I can get a job. Today is Mom's 38th birthday so my sisters and I made a quick surprise party for her when she got home.

May 22
I found out Payless won't let me work off the fine because of their insurance. Maybe I can get a job at Harrah's Casino to make money there.

Chet Stafford died today! It was so sad. Everyone on *The Guiding Light* was there. <u>Finally something happened</u>!

June 1

Monday. Today I had to go to school for a few tests and everyone was wondering where I'd been for the last two weeks. I told everyone that I was in the <u>hospital</u>. Nobody asked questions.

June 2

UPDATE: Only one more week till my shoplifting fine is due. I'm trying to sell my Walkman to Sean. I've been babysitting, and now I have $54.08 saved up.

June 8

I'm only $13.72 away from my $100 goal. The deadline is Wednesday <u>and</u> my Mom <u>still</u> doesn't even know. So far, so good. I didn't take the school bus home today; I cut my last class and walked home instead. They were throwing pee balloons because the water was shut off. It was a long walk, but at least I don't have pee on me.

Journal, I think I'm <u>different</u> than other people. I've only told this to my grandmother and my counselor Chuck. He said that I could be gay. Oh My God! <u>I think he's right!</u>

UPDATE: I have to go back to P.E. class next week <u>no matter what</u> and the school gave me two choices:

1. I can take adaptive, for like crippled children, or . . .
2. I can join the Cross Country Running Team (because they need people.)

I don't know <u>what</u> to do!

373

June 9

I asked Sean if he could loan me $14 (so I could buy my money order and send off the Payless fine). He wanted to know what it was for so I told him I needed it to go to New York and be on tour with Liza Minnelli . . . and <u>he believed me</u>! Now, my fine is all sent off now and I'm glad the whole thing is over!

I changed the name of the soap opera I'm writing from *Love of Nerd* to *No Life to Live*. The other name was stupid.

June 15

<u>BIG HUGE P.E. UPDATE!</u> I made a decision! I joined the Cross Country Team yesterday! All I have to do is run really fast through the forest.

Next year is going to be <u>SO</u> totally <u>cinchy</u>.

I haven't seen *The Guiding Light* in a LONG time. Oh well, no big.

June 18

Journal, Oh My God! Today my Mom said that I get to go see Aunt Liza <u>in concert</u> at the Paramount Theater in Seattle! I can't wait! To me, Aunt Liza is my favorite of everything.

I saw my counselor Chuck after school today for the last time. He says I have to start going to school <u>every</u> day, talking to people about my feelings, and over the summer, come up with a plan on making a better life. Wow.

June 19

Friday. I woke up today, and I cut school. I went to Payless and I stole a back scratcher and a TV band radio. I don't know why.

WACKIES

Michael Stern

At the age of seven, the most exciting thing in the world for me was a trip to the liquor store. Not to buy cigarettes or booze, but to get my hands on wax-coated trading cards like Wacky Packages and Garbage Pail Kids. They fascinated me.

Many dismissed these cards as juvenile. But they were in fact the brainchilds of respected artists like Art Spiegelman and Norman Saunders. The mixture of anticorporatism and scatological humor was an inspiration to me. I not only became an avid collector, but also created my *own* card series.

I called them Wackies . . . and they took potshots at everything from local media (the *Detroit Free Press*) to corporate behemoths (Kmart). Were these the height of creative expression for a seven-year-old? Or simply just mortifying? You pee the judge.

1, 1985

Dear Diary,
There is a hurricane
one and it's my only
in you just
anymore,
even scared
on them and
we have no p
everyone in my
that John Taylor
members of Dura
a voice in my

JESUS, JOHN, AND
HURRICANE GLORIA
Maria Victoria Suozzo

with you. I really ho
that EVERYONE including me are/is
especially John Taylor and the rest
Duran. Dear God please have mercy
atop the earth quakes, tornadoes,
es, tidal waves, famine, and
especially this PLEAS

I began writing in a diary shortly after I had my first Communion. However, it wasn't until a few years later, when Hurricane Gloria hit Long Island, that I began to use my diary for prayer.

September 27, 1985

Dear Diary,

There is a hurricane here. A very bad one and it's my only chance to write in you just in case I'm not around anymore. My mom and my step-dad are even scared too. The windows have tape on them and the trees are banging and we have no power.

I just hope that everyone in my family is all right and that John Taylor and all the other band members of Duran Duran are O.K. I've got a voice in myself that said I might be saving everyone's lives by writing now and that is why I want to write if that is all right with you. I really hope and pray that EVERYONE including me are/is all right, especially John Taylor and the rest of Duran Duran.

Dear God, please have mercy.

Please stop the earthquakes, tornados, hurricanes, tidal waves, famine, and all bad things, especially this PLEASE! Please save all of our lives! Please dear, DEAR Lord Jesus Christ! Really, help us all!

Please especially help John Taylor and may this writing help save him because I love him and I know that you love him too.

ADULT ME SAYS

As the years progressed and I entered my teens, my diary became a vessel through which I began to speak directly to God and ask for guidance in making major life-changing decisions.

December 20, 1988
Dear Diary,

I am so confused and I don't know what to do. I'm so scared about making the wrong choice and I don't know who to talk to because I'm afraid my friends will think I'm crazy, so I'm writing in you now, as if a pen and paper will actually have an answer for me. Oh my God I am so confused!!

For the past 7 years of my life I have been totally loyal to and madly in love with John Taylor of Duran Duran. I have 147 pictures of him and I have kissed every single one. I've only been able to see Duran Duran in concert once, but I know John saw me because he started doing the exact same dance move that I was doing! He's been in so many of my dreams since I first saw him in the video for "Planet Earth" when I was 6 and I loved him at first sight.

But now, dear God please help me, I am so confused because there is someone new. I didn't even know how much I liked this guy until he came to me in a dream last night. He held me and kissed me and sang to me and other things happened that I can't even write down, but I wanted to do them, I wanted to do everything and oh my God I'm so confused and he's so hot!

His name is Axl Rose.

Oh My God. He's got long red hair and leather pants and he told me he loved me! I know it was only a dream and John Taylor actually saw me in real life, but oh my God! Axl makes me feel crazy inside, even crazier than John Taylor, oh dear Lord I can't believe I just wrote that, but it's true! I'm so confused! What do I do?

Oh dear God please help me, please help me make the right choice! I mean, John lives in England and he only saw me that one time at Madison Square Garden, so maybe he forgot about me. And Axl used to be in the choir at church and I am going to Catholic school next year so we already have that in common. I mean, in my dream he told me that he wrote "Sweet Child O' Mine" for me. For me!

Dear God please help me, especially now because I need to tell my mom which tape I want for my Christmas stocking either Duran Duran "Big Thing" or Guns N' Roses "Appetite For Destruction."

Oh God, I know that I'm not really cheating on John Taylor by wanting Axl Rose so badly, but there! There, I said it! I do want him! I want Axl Rose! Oh dear God, but I just looked at my Duran Duran poster from "Hungry Like The Wolf" and John looks so hot and I feel so guilty!

Oh NO! Does that mean I'm a slut?!?!

I need to go to confession!

I'll write more later.

LAW OF THE LAND

Law Tarello

Most Italian-American boys growing up in Bensonhurst, Brooklyn, are either tough or feign some sort of tough-guy attitude.

I was sensitive, aware at a very young age that the world was a *big* place full of problems more significant than my own. Perhaps to ignore my *own* worries, I seemed to be worried about *everything else*.

And what better place to express my concern than in my homework assignments?

March 1984, 8 years old
ASSIGNMENT #1
Write a response to one of the articles we read last week in "Current Events."

To Whom It May Concern:

Last week I read a news story that Ringling Brothers Circus turned a goat into a unicorn. I think that is one of the meanest things you could do to a goat. Now his family won't recognize him and other goats will think he's weird. It was not nice to do this to him. How would you like it if I took your nose and put it in the middle of your forehead so people would pay money to look at you and laugh at you.

You wouldn't like it . . . so put the goat back to a goat. Thank you.

Teacher's note: Very good work! Please have your mother set up a parent-teacher conference!

April 1986, 10 years old
ASSIGNMENT #2

Write about something you hate and something you love.

I hate President Reagan. My mom says you should not say that you hate someone because that means you wish death upon them. I don't think it was right to bomb Libya.

Momar Kadaffy is a bad guy but innocent women and children died when bombs hit their houses. President Reagan did this and I hate him for it.

I love my grandpa Sal because he takes me and my cousins Michael and Matthew to movies and buys us pizza and takes out his teeth to scare us.

Teacher's note: Follow directions more carefully. The assignment was to write about something you hate and love, not someone. Please have your mother setup a parent-teacher conference.

ADULT ME SAYS

My mom later moved us from Brooklyn to a little town in upstate New York. I lost my friends. I lost my accent. But I never lost my strong opinions or refusal to back down.

My angst turned into activism, and again the only place I felt the need to express my disappointment with "the system" was during school hours. This is a letter I wrote to my homeroom teacher, who also happened to be my English teacher.

January 1991, 14 years old

Dear Ms. Truman,

I'm writing you this letter in response to your recommending me for a week of in-school-suspension. I don't understand. I explained that I only refuse to stand up and say the "Pledge of Allegiance" while we are at war and that I didn't know that was against school policy. So I apologized but you still sent me to Mr. Orcott's office. He said the rule was that as long as I stood up, I don't have to say the actual pledge.

You didn't even give me that option, you just sent me off to the principal's office like some criminal.

I thought you were one of the only people that understood me. And I know we're not peers and I do respect you as my teacher, but when you helped me with my audition for *Our Town* I felt like we connected.

Every time you ask the class for someone to read *Julius Caesar* and no one volunteers, who always does it . . . ME. And when you told me you were curious about rap music I lent you my only copy of *Licensed to Ill*, even though it was one of my favorite tapes (which, BTW, you have yet to return to me). And when you gave me that copy of *Leaves of Grass* before Christmas, I don't know, I just thought we were cool.

But now I can see that we're not cool. You are not cool.

Is this because your last name is Truman? Are you like related to Harry S. Truman or something and now you're taking it out on me? So, in conclusion, Ms. Truman—I don't want to be suspended therefore I will stand up but I won't say the pledge until the war is over.

And in the words of Walt Whitman " . . . I will make a song for the ears of the President, full of weapons with menacing points. And behind the weapons countless dissatisfied faces." Well Ms. Truman, you will have to see my dissatisfied face for 3 1/2 more years.

Sincerely,

Law Tarello

P.S. Seriously, I would like my Beastie Boys tape back by the end of the week.

WHAT THE HELL HAPPENED?

Alexa Alemanni currently works and resides in Los Angeles as an actress and a writer.

Carolyn Almos is an actress, writer, and part-time professor in Los Angeles. She has made humiliation her life's calling by cofounding Burglars of Hamm, a comedy company with a large repertoire of embarrassing plays. She no longer speaks with an accent.

Anne Altman lives in Manhattan, where she has a job in a building and sits in a chair at a desk. She entertains herself and others by writing and performing comedy. Visit annealtman.blogspot.com for information.

Anonymous is still in therapy and has been for years. She hopes to own up to her shady past *someday*, but unfortunately remains mortified until that day comes.

Brandy Barber is a writer and comedian living in Brooklyn, New York. Her articles have appeared in the pages of *BUST*, *Playgirl*, and *Time Out New York*. Read her stuff at brandyforsale.com.

Sara Barron grew up, had sex, and learned that peeing and orgasming are not the same thing—most of the time. Sara is a writer and performer in New York City. Visit sarabarron.com for information.

Cheryl Calegari is a stand-up comedian and comedy writer in New York City. To pay the bills, she is a PR and marketing executive . . . not for Chanel.

Qraig de Groot finally figured out what made him "the fat kid," lost more than one hundred pounds after college, and now lives a relatively healthy life in New Jersey, where he works in the music industry, writes on the side, exercises when he can, and still occasionally indulges in a bucket of fried chicken.

Hayley Downs is a documentary filmmaker living in Brooklyn, New York, with her fiancé, Marlan Barry. They have no pets.

Maggie Fine is a working actress who grew up in Santa Fe, New Mexico, and presently lives in Hollywood, California. She is also a partner in FineWill Productions and writes. Her relentless energy, self doubt, and periodic breakdowns continue to fuel her creativity and ability to connect with her characters.

Lori Fowler is currently going to school to become an elementary school teacher. Check out her website at skybirdsnplanes.com.

Jon Friedman is a comedian, writer, and comedy show producer from New York City. He is the creator and host of *The Rejection Show*, a variety show that features the rejected material of writers, comedians, cartoonists, artists, and everyday human folks. Jon's work and future projects can be found on the web at tremendousrabbit.com and at rejectionshow.com.

Jake Goldman is a television editor in New York City. He still has a terrible voice for hip-hop and writes on his odd website, internetdogfist.com.

Lori Gottlieb is the author of *I Love You, Nice To Meet You* (St. Martin's Press, 2006) and *Stick Figure: A Diary of My Former Self* (Simon & Schuster, 2000). A journalist and NPR commentator, she lives in Los Angeles with her newborn son, Zach, who shares her love of eating. Note: Portions of the text in this book book originally appeared in *Stick Figure*.

Stacey Grenrock Woods became a writer for *Esquire* and an actress on the *Daily Show* and *Arrested Development*. Her first book, *I California* (Scribner), a collection of funny essays, will be out in 2007.

Jillian Griffiths, a native New Yorker, resides full time in Los Angeles, where she has become embedded in the world of entertainment. Aside from acting and photography, she enjoys working in production, especially projects centered around the world of extreme sports. Noteworthy projects include *Step into Liquid* and *Dust to Glory*, with many more to come.

Kirsten Gronfield is an actor (*10 Items or Less* on TBS) and writer in Los Angeles. She cowrites, coproduces, and costars in *The Almost Grownups*, a sketch-hybrid show about trying to be an adult. Her eighth-grade self is so psyched to be published.

Adam Gropman is a writer, comedian, and actor living in Los Angeles. A short film he wrote and starred in was in the HBO Comedy Arts Festival in Aspen in 2006. Some of his various performing and writing ventures can be found at maximumlaughs.com. Adam is planning on doing a full one-man show about his camp experiences, titled *Unhappy Camper*.

Abby Gross is an editor in New York who teaches kids about current events via indykids.net.

Mathew Harawitz is a writer and comedian in Los Angeles. May his virginity rest in peace.

Brianna Jacobson is an aspiring writer and comedian in New York City. She is still waiting to meet Seth Green, although she doesn't know what she would say to him.

Sharone Jelden returned to her home state of Massachusetts after spending years in New York and Los Angeles. Now married and raising two children, she has lost the desire to live in poverty. Info at sharonejelden@comcast.net.

Anne Jensen is currently living in Los Angeles and is successfully pursuing a career in writing, acting, and singing. She eventually lost her weight (but not through Weight Watchers) and never hooked up with the main guy in her entries. She is the cowriter and costar of the hit comedy stage show *Almost Grown-Ups*. She also doesn't use Jesus or God anymore to get her dates. She uses her breasts. Love, Anne Jensen.

Blaise K has three careers: writing, Web design, and photography. (Four if you count hussy with a heart of gold.) She has performed in New York at P.S. 122, Bowery Poetry Club, and Lolita Bar. Explore her vanity projects at bazima.com.

Neil Katcher lives in Los Angeles and is a coproducer of *Mortified LA*. When he's not busy laughing at the angst of others, he's producing cable television, writing a feature documentary, directing for the stage, and occasionally penning a column for the *Jewish Journal of Greater Los Angeles*. In addition, he's a self-involved jerk who gets off on writing his own bio. His mother still loves him.

Christina Kerby is a public relations officer for San Francisco's water department. When she's not discussing water or raw sewage with the general public, her favorite pastime is telling embarrassing stories about herself to anyone who will listen.

Jennifer Kirmse is a filmmaker and comic genius who somehow wound up making video games for George Lucas. Visit reeltruthproductions.com to learn about her film, *Focus on Me*, which deals with her charming, developmentally disabled sister.

Krista Lanphear cowrote and costarred in *Material Girls*, a play inspired by her junior high immaturity. She also has the privilege of being a *Mortified* producer. Krista is an actor living in Los Angeles with the author. She loves him . . . and ice cream. No, seriously, she really loves them.

Keleigh Lanphear spends her days at a community college, counseling kids half her age, and her nights at hip clubs, hanging out with kids half her age. She's also just finished writing the eighth *Harry Potter* book.

Scott Lifton lives in San Francisco, where he helps heal the world by producing *Mortified SF*. He transferred his voyeurism into a budding producing career. He also waits tables. He's okay with that. In addition, he is *finally* maintaining a healthy relationship.

Gabriel Lopez was born and raised in the utopian, post-modern-experimental-capitalist-oriented-concrete-suburbia of Levittown on the island of Puerto Rico. El Señor López moved to Los Angeles to pursue a life in architecture. In order to make a better world, he split his time between the pursuit of architectural perfection and polishing his anecdotes—both influential on his physical and spiritual baldness.

Jennifer McDonnell is a Web producer living in Santa Monica. She continues to record her daily life at JennChantal.com. To this day, Jennifer has never smoked a cigarette.

Vanessa Murdock lives in Toronto with her two cats and boyfriend. She works in TV program acquisitions and is proud to be a part of bringing *90210* back to Canada (the original *OC*, baby). She loves dancing all night and hates green peppers.

Rylan Morrison designs jewelry and performs improv comedy. Her jewelry can be seen at whitelimo.blogspot.com, and she can be seen performing regularly at the Magnet Theater in New York City.

David Nadelberg totally likes you. He encourages *everyone* to dig up their past and share it with just one other person. It's a strangely rewarding experience. Oh, and he created *Mortified* (getmortified.com) and writes and stuff.

Will Nolan is "gay for pay," managing Wilderness Media & Entertainment, a gay and lesbian portfolio company that among other things produces the nationally syndicated *Radio with a Twist*. He lives just outside of New York City with his husband, Stephen. They are awaiting the arrival of their first child.

Niya Palmer is a Los Angeles-based comedy writer. With oodles of therapy she was able to enjoy this past February for the first time in years.

Mark Phinney is an actor and writer barely surviving in Los Angeles.

Retta graduated from Duke University with a degree in sociology with pre-med requirements fulfilled. She now lives in Los Angeles working as a stand-up comedienne and actress. She is making absolutely no use of her degree.

Sascha Rothchild is a TV writer in Los Angeles. She gave up her slutty ways and got married. But she still does coke every day just to make sure she's not addicted.

Giulia Rozzi is a writer and comedic performer, splitting her time between Boston and New York City, where she coproduces *Mortified*. She also travels to campuses, educating students about body and food issues. You can find out more at giuliarozzi.com.

Jami Rudofsky is a casting director in Los Angeles and lives with her dogs, Ella and Tallulah.

Stephen Scaia finally abandoned his dreams of becoming the greatest fighter pilot in the history of the U.S. Navy, becoming a television writer instead. His mother is very proud, regardless. He lives in Los Angeles.

Ari Scott is a musician living in New York City. She takes classes in long-form improvisation and likes to make her website (ariscott.com) pretty.

Victoria Scroggins now lives in Brooklyn while attending film school at Brooklyn College. Someday she will write and direct an amazing film, but for now she spends a lot of time with her dog, Pinkerton, and her girlfriend, Caroline (yes, the one from her story). The author would also like to state that upon reviewing this entry years later, she feels a need to say that Katherine [a pseudonym] is, in fact, not crazy, and is one of the most awesome people in the world. The two are friends (we'll see after the publishing of the entry; keep your fingers crossed).

Will Seymour has managed to scratch his way to the middle and eke out a career as an unknown actor and writer. All the details can be perused, mocked, and debated with a click to williamseymour.com. Update: Liza Minnelli kept all her promises and turned out to be a most amazing woman, with great advice and a generous soul.

Michael Stern is still entertaining himself with fart jokes and bad puns. He lives in San Diego, California, and writes.

Maria Victoria Suozzo currently lives in Queens, New York, with her fiancé, who is sweet enough to occasionally don leather pants and a red wig just to keep her on her toes.

Law Tarello currently resides in New York City with his wife, Kathleen. He is a "working" actor/improv comic. For proof of this, feel free to visit lawtarello.com.